D0908830

# IMPUTED RIGHTS

*An Essay in Christian Social Theory*

ROBERT V. ANDELSON

# IMPUTED RIGHTS

··{ *An Essay in Christian Social Theory* }··

For. Dr. Thos. A. Gaskin, III
with sincere appreciation
and regards.
                    Rob V. Andelson

1-15-79

University of Georgia Press, Athens

Library of Congress Catalogue Card Number: 70–135183
Standard Book Number: 8203–0270–8

The University of Georgia Press, Athens 30601

Printed in the United States of America
by The TJM Corporation
Baton Rouge, Louisiana 70821

To my Mother

This liberty of our own actions is such a fundamental privilege of human nature that God Himself, notwithstanding all His infinite power and right over us, permits us to enjoy it, and that too after a forfeiture made by the rebellion of Adam.

—*Abraham Cowley*

# Contents

# Foreword

In our modern confusion about the meanings of words,
most people are at sea when they come upon such terms
as "natural rights," "natural law," "rights of man,"
"human rights," "chartered rights of men," and "higher
law." Yet justice cannot be attained until a proper understanding of these terms is restored. Professor Robert
V. Andelson's book is a courageous endeavor to renew
the metaphysical foundations of natural rights. Knowing
that all differences of opinion are theological at bottom,
Mr. Andelson reaffirms the religious understanding of
human nature, natural law, and natural right.

For natural rights to be recognized, there must be
postulated an immutable human nature and a body of
moral law pertaining to that nature. Some serious writ-
ing on this large subject has appeared in recent years—
the books of A. P. d'Entrevès, Leo Strauss, John C. H.
Wu, and Peter Stanlis, among others. Robert Andelson
relates the doctrine of natural rights to the Christian
teaching about man and to many of our present discon-
tents. Concerning the interpretation of natural rights,
men always will differ: I happen to agree with many of
Mr. Andelson's particular interpretations, but to dissent
from other interpretations of his. However this may be,
it is Andelson's achievement to remind us of the sound

and true basis for those rights which are not conferred by positive law.

Natural right flows from natural law. As a term of jurisprudence and politics, natural law may be defined as a loosely-knit body of rules of action prescribed by an authority superior to the state. These rules are presumed to be derived from divine intent, from the nature of man, or from the long experience of man in community.

On the one hand, natural law and natural right must be distinguished from positive or statutory law, decreed by the state; on the other, from the "laws of nature" in a scientific sense—that is, from propositions expressing the regular order of certain natural phenomena. The most cogent early treatise on natural law and the rights derived from that law is Cicero's *De Re Publica*—although those concepts may be found in Plato and earlier writers. This Ciceronian understanding of natural law, mingled in later centuries with Christian thought, was well expressed in the nineteenth century by Froude: "Our human laws are but the copies, more or less imperfect, of the eternal laws so far as we can read them, and either succeed and promote our welfare, or fail and bring confusion and disaster, according as the legislator's insight has detected the true principle, or has been distorted by ignorance or selfishness."

As interpreted by the Roman jurisconsults, and later by the medieval Schoolmen and Canonists, the legacy of the classical *ius naturale* experienced little challenge until the seventeenth century. From Sophocles' *Antigone* and Aristotle's *Ethics* and *Rhetoric*, through the Stoic philosophers of Hellenistic and Roman times, a continuity runs until the beginnings of secularism and rationalism in the seventeenth century. Until the middle of that century, in the Christian world, the natural law was believed to be a body of unwritten rules depending on a transcendent insight of the human race, on universal conscience, and on common sense; it was closely connected, from the triumph of Christianity onward, with

Christian moral teachings. In the words of Sir Ernest Barker, "This justice is conceived as being the higher or ultimate law, proceeding from the nature of the universe —from the Being of God and the reason of man. It follows that law—in the sense of the law of the last resort—is somehow above law-making."

Natural rights, derived from this body of natural law, were understood to be immunities and privileges essential to the fulfillment of divine intent for man: rights enabling the human creature to realize full humanity, in the image of God. (In the phrase of a twentieth-century writer, Stefan Andreas, "We are God's Utopia.") If denied these rights, the human being would be something less than what divine wisdom intended him to be.

Late in the seventeenth century, however, a secularized and rationalistic interpretation of natural law appeared, conspicuous in the works of Hugo Grotius and Samuel von Pufendorf. This latter concept of natural law was embraced by many of the *philosophes* of the eighteenth century, and took flesh during the French Revolution, when it was popularized by Thomas Paine. So were conceived the abstract "Rights of Man," unrelated either to divine providence or to historical experience.

Yet the older understanding of natural law was not extinguished. In part, Immanuel Kant sustained it. It was ringingly asserted by Edmund Burke, in his distinction between the "real" and the "pretended" rights of men. Here Burke stood in the tradition of Richard Hooker, and, more remotely, of the Schoolmen and of Cicero.

During the nineteenth century, concepts of natural law and natural right were overshadowed by the powerful utilitarian system of Jeremy Bentham, by the theories of John Austin and the Analytical Jurists, by legal positivism, and later—particularly in America—by legal pragmatism. The collapse of the Enlightenment's structure of rationalistic "natural law" was thought by many to involve in its ruin the earlier natural-law and natural-right tradition from which the Enlightenment's "natural law" had deviated.

In the United States the older and newer schools of natural-law theory have contended confusedly against each other since the latter half of the eighteenth century, and both have been strongly assailed by positivistic, utilitarian, and pragmatic interpretations of law. Yet appeals to the "natural law" and "natural right," or to a "higher law," have recurred often in American politics and jurisprudence; both conservatives and radicals, on occasions, have invoked the rights ordained from nature.

The difficulty of defining natural law and natural right, and of discovering clear sactions, involves these doctrines in controversy. A. P. d'Entrevès writes, "The doctrine of natural law is in fact nothing but an assertion that law is a part of ethics." Yet, he concludes, "The lesson of natural law [is] simply to remind the jurist of his own limitations. . . . This point where values and norms coincide, which is the ultimate origin of law and at the same time the beginning of moral life proper, is, I believe, what men for over two thousand years have indicated by the name of natural law."

Robert Andelson agrees with Professor d'Entrevès that values and norms coincide in natural law and natural right; but he affirms a more coherent metaphysical foundation for this justice than does d'Entrevès. Rejecting the rationalists' and the utilitarians' theories of the foundation of law and right, Mr. Andelson offers us a renewed apprehension of the transcendent consciousness of ordered freedom. The service of God is perfect freedom: this is no paradox, for both our personal and our social nature proceed from God.

Russell Kirk

Mecosta, Michigan
November 1970

# Preface

This book is an outgrowth of a doctoral study which I did in the late 1950s at the University of Southern California under the guidance of a committee headed by Professor Harvey J. D. Seifert. The academic world is full of people who call themselves liberal but who automatically downgrade any student who does not share their bias. Only one who has been the victim of such arrogance can adequately appreciate the genuine liberalism of Dr. Seifert and his colleagues on the committee, Professors Donald H. Rhoades and Wilbert L. Hindman. They encouraged me to pursue the topic of my choice, knowing that I brought to it an orientation radically at variance with many of their own beliefs. And when, after they had gently forced me (as was right) to come to grips with the arguments for those beliefs, my pursuit eventuated in conclusions largely hostile to their personal predilections and commitments, their helpfulness abated not one whit. It was for persons such as they, I think, that the expression "gentlemen and scholars" must have been invented.

The dissertation, a typological study of the concept of human rights, was completed in 1960 with the aid of a fellowship from the Foundation for Social Research, for which it gives me pleasure to express indebtedness. I soon resolved to recast the work for publication, omitting most of the historical analysis, and developing my own position more fully. Leisure to accomplish this did not come until 1967, when a grant from the Relm Foundation afforded me a respite from my classroom obligations. To this body, and especially to its secretary, Mr. Richard A. Ware, I wish to acknowledge my profound gratitude. Auburn University generously provided a supplemental grant for secretarial and research expenses. In this connection I should be remiss if I failed to mention the kindness of Dr. Ben T. Lanham, Jr., vice-president for research, who extended to me the active cooperation of his office in other ways as well.

*Imputed Rights* might never have become a reality had it not been for the counsel and encouragement of two highly esteemed friends, the Reverend Mr. Edmund A. Opitz and Professor M. E. Bradford. Thanks are due to several other friends who read the manuscript either in full or in part and gave me the benefit of their comments: Professors Bernard R. Breyer, William H. Davis, and Madison P. Jones (all of Auburn University) , and the Reverend Messrs. John Kuykendall and Rousas J. Rushdoony. Its faults, of course, are my responsibility alone, and I hasten to absolve Dr. Davis and Mr. Kuykendall of any suspicion that they endorse its general socio-political thrust.

George Core, editor of the University of Georgia Press, warned me that he would be cranky, but I found him as gracious and sympathetic as I could have wished. The typescript was most efficiently prepared by Mrs. Edward Wegener, who also assisted ably in the compilation of the index.

Finally, I wish to pay tribute to the patience of my wife, Bonny, whose willingness to put up with my irascibility and preoccupation is but one of the many reasons why I am devoutly grateful that she is my life companion.

Auburn, Alabama                                   R. V. A.
Summer, 1970

# Prolegomena

Today insistent forces press for social change, demanding ascendency in the name of human rights. The civil rights movement, the anti-poverty crusade, the assault upon colonialism, the campaigns for academic freedom, military disengagement, birth control—all engender passionate involvement and give frequent rise to admirable impulses of self-sacrifice and courage. Yet all this activism has not been accompanied by any corresponding effort to clarify intellectually the concept which it claims to serve. Concern for rights animates heroic combat volunteers not less than those who march in peace parades, last-ditch resistance to the power of centralized authority not less than the employment of that power to lift the status of aggrieved minorities, opposition to compulsory unionism not less than agitation for workers' solidarity, zeal for strengthening law enforcement not less than fastidiousness for due process, the *National Review* not less than the *New Republic*. Plainly, there is confusion somewhere! All honor to the motives of those who sincerely demonstrate for rights as they best understand them. But perhaps what is most needed now is less demonstrating and more hard thinking about precisely what it is that constitutes a right.

The modern temper is not friendly to theoretical disquisitions on the nature of justice. One hears it said that such efforts are a waste of time, that mankind is in fundamental accord as to what is meant by justice, and that the area of disagreement lies in the question of what means are to be utilized in attaining it. If one takes seriously the sloganry of propagandists, this contention has a degree of surface plausibility: freedom, security, and the good life are proclaimed as human rights by politicians of every ideological stripe and hue. But the vacuity of such sloganry becomes quickly evident when one considers that for Hitler the term "human" had a racially delimited sphere of application, that by "freedom" Mussolini meant self-realization through submission to the state, that the "security" enforced by Trujillo was that of a prison or a graveyard, and that the Marxist concept of "the good life" is best epitomized by the symbol of an ant-heap.

The fact is that theoretical considerations are of crucial importance in determining both ends and means in politics and jurisprudence. When an Ataturk decrees the abolition of the fez, or a Nehru the extirpation of untouchability, decisions have been made which reflect a profound revolution in ends. When the United States Constitution is amended to allow for a graduated federal income tax, or interpreted to outlaw racial segregation in the public schools, dramatic changes in philosophic world-view have become manifest.

Frank Knight has remarked, "The differences between men which give rise to serious conflict rest in differences of opinion about rights rather than mere clashes of individual 'selfish' interest." [1] While this is perhaps an overstatement, it rests upon a sound and valid insight.

This essay is an attempt to get at the heart of the problem of just what it is that makes rights rights. This is a problem which has been surprisingly neglected.[2] Much has been written about specific rights but relatively little with any philosophical pretension about rights in general. Such technical literature as does exist is mostly of the critical variety which seeks to undermine the theory of natural rights but which does not substitute for it any kind of criterion not subject to the vagaries of time and place.

My approach assumes quite frankly a theological frame of reference. It will not convince, nor was it intended to convince, positivists or humanists; it was undertaken to provide serious Christians with a doctrine of rights rigorously in keeping with the theocentric basis of their piety. On first consideration, such an effort may appear superfluous, for invocation of the name of God is scarcely rare in proclamations of the rights of man, nor is Christian literature affirming human rights unusual. Yet such invocation cannot commonly be understood as more than honorific, and such affirmation cannot commonly be clearly seen as something which follows logically from the premises asserted. Christian affirmations of the rights of man betray, almost monotonously, a rationale which contradicts fundamental Christian tenets, a rationale unconsciously borrowed from humanism, whether of the Classical or the Enlightenment variety.

Since even Christian theories of human rights have, in fact, for the most part depended upon essentially secular arguments, the question may be raised as to why a theocentric view of human rights is needed. Can this topic not be adequately dealt with from a frame of reference based on common ground, one which does not require any more ultimate agreement than a shared concern for human welfare? My answer to this question is twofold: first of all, it must be said that although a concern for human welfare is indeed implicit in the Christian faith, any effort to translate it directly into the language of rights will founder on the doctrine of the Fall of Man, which renders untenable any simple deduction of rights from the order of creation. Despite Mr. Jefferson's rhetoric, there is from the Christian standpoint nothing self-evident in the proposition that all (or indeed, any) men are endowed with unalienable rights. No view of human rights which fails to take thoroughgoing account of man's fallen nature can be considered consonant with the demands of normative Christian theology—or, for that matter, even of psychological realism. Secondly, as I shall now attempt to demonstrate, only a theocentric position can provide a really secure anchor for the concept.

． ． ．

A careful review of salient theories of human rights reveals three great traditions into which they fall when analyzed in terms of ground, end, and regulating principle. To these may be assigned the names "radical-humanist," "utilitarian," and "metaphysical," respectively. They are, at bottom, mutually exclusive, although since they are ideal types and therefore necessarily abstractions few if any individual theorists represent any one of them with absolute consistency.

The radical-humanist tradition deduces rights from an uncritical veneration of man *qua* man. Its ground is a romantic view of man, its end is freedom, and its regulating principle, equality.

The utilitarian tradition holds that rights are nothing but pragmatic fictions. Its ground is a hedonistic view of man, its end is quantitative happiness, and its regulating principle, expediency. The utilitarian orientation is not to be confused with mere cynicism, such as the contention of Thrasymachus that justice is the interest of the stronger,[3] or the nihilistic declamations of Max Stirner.[4] Such purely negative positions constitute not a theory of rights but a flat denial of their existence. The utilitarian tradition, on the other hand, always assumes the "greatest happiness principle" as its ultimate sanction, although this is often implicit rather than spelled out.

The metaphysical tradition derives rights from man's place in a purposive order. Its ground is a view of man as related to something higher than himself, its end is cosmic purpose, and its regulating principle, function. Within this tradition two sub-categories may be distinguished, according to whether the content of its formal end be interpreted as personal fulfillment or the intrinsically authoritative will of God. The first of these comprises the various self-realization theories of human rights, such as those which stem from classical humanism and modern philosophical idealism. The second comprises theories which seek to clarify the implications of theonomy for human rights and which are rooted largely in that strand of Christian thought which may be loosely characterized as the Reformed perspective. The object of the present work is to develop a theory of this type, building chiefly upon foundations laid by Calvin—foundations upon which, in my opinion, despite some efforts of solid and enduring worth, no balanced superstructure has been squarely hitherto erected.

Heretofore, radical-humanist and metaphysical theories have usually been lumped together under the generic heading of "natural rights theories." Yet it must be recognized that by the eighteenth century natural rights had come to be regarded as ends in themselves, rather than as necessary means to the fulfillment of man's proper destiny in a telic universe. This discontinuity would seem to call for the division of natural rights theories into two discrete categories, as I have done.

The radical-humanist tradition is, by virtue of its artificiality and lack of functional relatedness, a sorry guarantor of human rights, for it is incapable of maintaining a stable equilibrium between its end and its regulating principle. Freedom, however precious, cannot be itself the end of human life. It remains empty and ultimately meaningless unless harnessed to the service of some further purpose. Whenever an attempt is made to give it content, freedom as an end turns into something other than itself. This accounts for the instability of the tradition. In the hands of Locke, for instance, it takes on a utilitarian coloration tinged with traces of Calvinism; in the hands of Rousseau, its tendency is metaphysical. But always it remains ambiguous. Contradiction is the essence of its nature, and it can achieve consistency only at the cost of its own existence. Moreover, radical-humanism misconstrues the concept of equal freedom. Instead of seeing equal freedom as the concrete means whereby the regulating principle of function is implemented, it makes freedom the end and equality the regulating principle. This destroys the tension between freedom and equality. Either equality, unrelated to function, ceases to serve merely as the regulating principle, and threatens to usurp the place of end as well, or freedom, unrelated to purpose, displaces equality as the regulating principle, while itself remaining formally the end. In the first case leveling collectivism is the outcome; in the second case, anarchy. But since neither freedom nor equality is viable as ultimate ends, anarchy has never been sustained as a deliberate system, and egalitarian collectivism has always eventuated in the subordination of equality as a final goal either to some pragmatic compromise or to some embodiment of the metaphysical ethos of the collectivity. This is seen clearly in the French Revolution, out of which arose both the Directory and Napoleon. The recent conflict in Red China between Liu Shao-chi and Mao Tse-tung was basically a struggle between these two alternatives.

Radical-humanism in the Lockean vein informed that concept of human rights reflected in the Constitution of the United States. Yet, while its framers for the most part veered toward deism in their personal theological convictions, they continued to retain the psychological and moral impress of Geneva. Lord Bryce remarks that "there is a hearty Puritanism in the view of human nature which pervades the instrument of 1787. It is the work of men who believed in original sin, and were resolved to leave open for transgressors no door which they could possibly shut." [5] But once severed from its spiritual moorings, it was only a matter of time before the natural rights dogma fell prey to the corrosive influences of positivism and historicism. For the better part of a century, the Lockean mythos, given juristic formulation by Sir William Blackstone and embodied in such principles as "due process" and "vested rights," shaped the dicta and decisions of the highest judicial authorities in the land—men like Chancellor Kent, Judge Cooley, and Justices Story, Field, Brewer, and Harlan. Yet all of this was nothing but inertia—the lingering echo of a lute long laid aside. And so eventually it came to pass that, in the somber judgment of Haines,

> the doctrine of the higher law or of fundamental principles as a basis to be applied to the amending procedure of the federal Constitution is seldom advocated. American legal thought more commonly follows the doctrine that there are no inalienable rights, that legal rights exist only through law, and that such a thing as a right in any legal sense against the sovereign political authority is unthinkable.[6]

"Political liberty," writes Edmund A. Opitz, "is a check drawn against the capital stock of our religious heritage. When the check bounces the inference is that there are no funds in the bank." [7]

In France the radical-humanist idea found dominant expression in the teaching of Rousseau, who stripped it of both the vestiges of Puritanism and the anticipations of utilitarianism with which it had been partly clothed by Locke, and impregnated it with the myth of the general will, dynamic germ of a false and vicious teleology. In Rousseau's *Social Contract* one finds the doctrine of natural rights bent to the service of totalitarian collectivism. It asserts that "the social order is a sacred right which is the basis of all other rights," and then explains that this order consists of

> . . . the total alienation of each associate, together with all his rights, to the whole community. . . . Each man, in giving himself to all, gives himself to nobody; and as there is no associate over which he does not acquire the same rights as he yields others over himself, he gains an equivalent for everything he loses, and an increase of force for the preservation of what he has.[8]

Sir Ernest Barker has admirably exposed the fallacy of this line of reasoning:

I surrender all of myself—and I surrender it all to 999 others as well as myself; I only receive a fraction of the sovereignty of the community; and ultimately I must reflect that if I am the thousandth part of a tyrant, I am also the whole of a slave.[9]

Rousseau would enslave men to ensure their freedom; in fact, "Freedom is Slavery," the sinister slogan of Orwell's *1984*, is simply an aphoristic echo from the *Social Contract*. "Whosoever refuses to obey the general will shall be compelled to do so by the whole body. This means nothing less than that he will be forced to be free." [10] Proceeding from an abstract view of natural rights, yet slipping almost imperceptibly into a rationale for one of the most brutal and hideous ochlocracies the world has ever known, the spirit of the *Social Contract* came to ominous flower when Robespierre announced, as spokesman for the Jacobins: "Our will is the general will."

Freedom cannot be either justified or long preserved except in terms of what Lord Acton so eloquently speaks of as "the equal claim of every man to be unhindered in the fulfillment by man of duty to God—a doctrine laden with storm and havoc, which is the secret essence of the Rights of Man." [11] Rights are not the simple patrimony of the human race but are instead concomitants to duties owed to God. They cannot be derived directly from natural law, for natural law was broken with the Fall of Man. Their title must be sought rather in the order of grace, wherein the law of nature is regenerated and restored. This is an insuperable stumbling-block to radical-humanism, and is the deepest reason why eighteenth-century rationalism, for all its polite gesture to a Supreme Being, never could provide an ethic sufficiently profound to adequately undergird its gospel of human rights.

This philosophy built no solid foundation for the rights of the human person because nothing can be founded on illusion: it compromised and squandered these rights, because it led men to conceive them as rights in themselves divine, hence infinite, escaping every objective measure, denying every limitation imposed upon the claims of the ego, and ultimately expressing the absolute independence of the human subject and a so-called absolute right—which supposedly pertains to everything in the human subject by the mere fact that it is in him—to unfold one's cherished possibilities at the expense of all other beings. When men thus instructed clashed on all sides with the impossible, they came to believe in the bankruptcy of the rights of the human person.[12]

The utilitarian tradition is no more coherent than is the radical-humanist. The psychological hedonism which is its ground is not demonstrably compatible with its end of quantitative happiness, for on the basis of the empirical method which it presupposes, utilitarianism is unable to show why, if men always seek their own pleasure and avoid their own pain, the greatest happiness of the greatest number can or should be the only proper end of conduct. It is incumbent upon the moralist who holds that individuals are invariably guided by self-interest and that the rightful end of human action is the general maximization of happiness, to provide conclusive evidence that the individual's felicity and that of the whole are ultimately the same. If he cannot do this, he sets forth a goal which may be impossible to realize because it is contrary to human nature. On the other hand, if such a demonstration could be made, the position would boil down to the assertion that everyone inevitably does what he ought to do, in which case the services of a moralist would appear to be superfluous. As for utilitarianism's regulating principle, expediency, it devolves in practice into sheer majoritarianism, inasmuch as the tradition excludes any qualitative criterion either for the valuation of different kinds of happiness or for the discrimination between individuals as to their capacity for the enjoyment thereof. Thus this philosophy, when not modified by other influences, leads undeviatingly to the domination of mere numbers.

It is by no means patent that there are sufficient hedonistic sanctions for virtuous conduct in this present life—if conduct based upon such sanctions can be, in any case, considered virtuous. Paley's theological utilitarianism solved this problem formally by dragging in God as a sort of mechanical device for providing a license for self-interest and a guarantee of its ultimate automatic harmony with the interests of the whole. Bentham, in contrast, prided himself upon his secularization of ethics, thinking that by practically ignoring the theological dimension he was imparting to the discipline a strictly scientific and empirical character. But in order to be logically tenable, even on a superficial level, utilitarianism requires a supernatural referent. Torn between two dogmas (the universality of the egoistic motive, and the greatest good of the greatest number) the commensurability of which is so dubious that their reconciliation depends upon the assumption that accounts are to be balanced in a hereafter, with the dissolution of the sacerdotal bond so despised by Bentham, the whole framework of utilitarianism disintegrates like the wings of Icarus in the sun.

Not only is "the greatest good [or happiness] of the greatest number" not otherwise demonstrably compatible with egoism, but it cannot really be equated with the greatest quantity of good. Long before the time of Bentham, the final quintessence of the utilitarian position was apodictically enunciated by Caiaphas: "It is expedient that one man should die for the sake of the people." [13] This is the natural conclusion of any system which assumes that "each one is to count for one, and no one for more than one," and which makes quantity of happiness its end. A viable theory of human rights requires that individuals be regarded as unique centers of value rather than as mere ciphers. It is instructive to note that Francis Hutcheson, who had first stated the greatest happiness principle, expressly qualified it by pointing out that "the dignity, or moral importance of Persons, may compensate numbers." [14] Bentham, however, was so indifferent to such considerations that he went on record as being quite willing that men should be transformed into robots by the application of his pedagogical techniques. ". . . Call them machines, so they were but happy ones, I should not care." [15]

Perhaps the most trenchant contemporary presentation of the utilitarian approach to human rights is to be found in Cornelia Geer LeBoutillier's *American Democracy and Natural Law*. Its thesis is that rights are best protected if separated from undemonstrable ideal foundations and made to rest frankly upon "the Greatest Happiness Principle sought by the pragmatic method." [16]

> Why must we "fly to the will of God" for explanation—in a political issue surely "the refuge of ignorance"? Why call the law of nature an expression of divine will when it can adequately be explained as human will? This pedestrian explanation is both more satisfying intellectually and more profitable in terms of human understanding and human good.[17]

Mrs. LeBoutillier believes that the experience of the race attests that freedom is essential to human happiness, and that "natural law, insofar as it is meaningful at all, is a word which has been used to name something easily verifiable in history, something undying in the human race: the insistent choice of freedom, even at high cost." [18] But here she is trapped by her own premises, for if empirical analysis be applied to the option of the greatest number, it would seem that servitude has a better claim than freedom to the title of human right. The "insistent choice of freedom" may be "easily verifiable in history," but only as a minority choice: free commonwealths from the Israel of the Judges to the Weimar Republic have fallen again and again because the overwhelming masses of men throughout the ages have been convinced that their happiness demands that they be subject to a caesar. According to every pragmatic test conceivable to me, the Grand Inquisitor's "unanimous and harmonious ant-heap" is the perfect epitome of a social order directed exclusively toward the goal of quantitative happiness.

Freedom is an aristocratic value, replete with pain and peril. Those who seek it as a means to happiness must be sooner or later disillusioned. Only those few who claim it for consecrated use in the service of transcendent good are justified in steadfastly accepting the suffering it brings. Yet nothing else is functionally deserving to be called a right.

Therefore, it is to the metaphysical tradition that we must turn for a satisfactory frame of reference, and within that tradition to a theonomous approach. For self-realization theories are inherently idolatrous and self-defeating. Self-realization, moralists have long observed, only comes as a by-product of the pursuit of other goals. When made itself the end of human rights, it issues in a eudaemonism which tends to elevate relative values into artificial absolutes as vehicles whereby the self attains fulfillment. Paradoxically, however, if such values—family, community, state, race, species, etc.—remain to the consciousness mere vehicles, they cannot function psychologically as absolutes, and therefore have no power even as vehicles. If, on the other hand, they come to be held as absolutes indeed, they lead to a distorted integration of the psyche which is actually a morbid parody of true fulfillment. The self can find but mechanical fulfillment as a member of a larger organism which supersedes and overwhelms it, for under such conditions it cannot really be a self. Selfhood occurs only within the realm of genuine personal relations, where the individual becomes an "I" in free, disinterested response to the address of "Thou." But such response must be initiated by the reconciling act of God, apart from which every "Thou" is valued only as a serviceable object. Without this reconciling act, even close familial ties are stifling and oppressive, even love is but a mask for parasitical emotional dependence. Authentic personality presupposes authentic community, but authentic community presupposes liberation from the trammels of self-preoccupation—liberation which cannot be achieved but only accepted through redemptive encounter with the Supreme "Thou," who draws us to Himself because He is Himself.[19]

It is in the Reformation ethos, with its stress upon the themes of justification, election, and the glory of God as the end of human existence, that theonomy finds least ambiguous expression. By recapturing the Pauline understanding of the meaning of grace, the Reformation uncompromisingly set in harsh relief the terrible pervasiveness of man's fallen state, which had been softened and obscured by the medieval synthesis of classical and Biblical ideas which came to flower in the majestic system of St. Thomas Aquinas.

The contemporary Thomist, Jacques Maritain, has eloquently indicted radical-humanism for its failure to see that only the fact of functional duty in terms of an order grounded in divine will provides a sound and stable basis for belief in human dignity and rights.[20] But in the course of an entire book in which the indictment is made he never once alludes to the problem posed by man's fallen nature, which stultifies the capacity to participate in that order save through God's justifying condescension. In this he but illustrates the inability of Thomism to come to grips with the full implications of the Fall. According to St. Thomas, the Adamic sin did not deprive man of his essential nature, but of a "super added gift," the blessedness of communion with his Maker.[21] As Wilhelm Pauck once remarked in a classroom lecture at which I was present, for Thomism "empirical man equals man minus the plus." That is, he lost something which was never really part of his nature in the first place. Thus, although sin may blur the image of God in man, it destroys nothing which pertains to temporal existence. Instead of viewing the creation as perverted and condemned save for the imputed worth of Christ, the Thomist outlook issues in a sacramentalism in which, as Reinhold Niebuhr puts it,

the natural world (including, unfortunately, the social orders of human history) is celebrated as the handiwork of God; and every natural fact is rightly seen as an image of the transcendent, but wrongly covered so completely with the aura of sanctity as to obscure its imperfections.[22]

Although he cannot now attain to supernatural and eternal bliss apart from special grace, man stands otherwise virtually as if the Fall had never taken place: his social rights and duties are vindicated on the basis of natural law, given in creation. These features are reflected in a highly optimistic view of the possibilities for rational life in society—a view which underestimates the irrational, demonic forces which have always constituted a dominant factor to be reckoned with in collective human relationships. They are also reflected in static and paternalistic predilections, stemming from a tendency to absolutize institutions of the thirteenth century by identifying them with natural orders established in creation.

The giants of the Reformation were not interested in the rights of man as such, and in practice their zeal was more likely to be ranged against than for the freedom of the individual. Yet, without necessarily intending it, they initiated an outlook which provides a genuine point of departure for a functional and evangelical view of human rights. For in proclaiming the rights of God over men, they also proclaimed by implication the rights of men vis-a-vis each other. Their doctrine is centered in the concept of vocation, to which Calvin gave a dynamic twist, replete with incendiary possibilities.

Luther saw the concept of vocation in a dualistic light. On the one hand, the secular estates, although differing in dignity, are equally ordained by God. The Christian is to abide with docility in the station to which he is called by birth. On the other hand, the priestly calling is no longer viewed as the exclusive possession of a sacerdotal class, but is rather something which consecrates internally the lives and occupations of the humblest believers by imbuing them with the impetus to loving service.

When the Peasants' Revolt sought to make the common priesthood of all Christians the excuse for the redress of secular abuses, Luther's reaction was one of wrath and horror. But the peasants were not amiss in discerning that the priestly calling which Luther extended to all believers carries with it basic rights correlative to the priestly function of service to the neighbor. Such rights do not, of course, necessitate the obliteration of external distinctions among Christians. But they do involve the objective freedom without which service is mere serfdom and access to those natural goods without which formal freedom is a hollow joke and service ultimately impossible. This is really all the peasants asked for: their "Twelve Articles" revolved around the two key demands of abolition of forced labor and restoration of common lands to the community. Luther's failure to derive from his doctrine its natural implication with respect to rights may probably be attributed to his abysmal pessimism regarding human nature and the world, which was not balanced by other considerations as in Calvin. The Christian, for Luther, lives in the midst of a world beyond redemption short of Christ's second coming; his own sanctification in this life is only rudimentary and quite subordinate to his status in the life beyond. In his capacity as a citizen of this fallen world, he participates in hierarchies and orders which, although divinely instituted, have no saving quality but are merely dikes against chaos. They are to be accepted as the punishment and restraint of sin. So vocation easily becomes a call to obedient labor in one's inherited station in society, coupled with a mandate to serve one's neighbor in ways spontaneously dictated by the opportunities of the time and place. The possibility of a rationalized social structure deduced from Christian premises is denigrated in favor of a fatalistic acceptance of the status quo. This attitude, evoked by an overmastering sense of human sinfulness and intellectual corruption, is related to a pronounced irrationalism and contempt for "system building," also characteristic of most "Neoorthodox" theologians of the present day.

Actually, Luther's teaching is not without certain tentative motions toward a different outlook altogether. As Brunner comments, there is no trace in the following citation of the stress on blind obedience usually attributed to

Luther: "Therefore shall not man let himself and his be forced into idolatry and false worship, but shall defend himself against it with *force* as long as he can. For obedience is to God and not to man." [23] But this represents the exceptional in Luther's teaching. He did not secularize the right of resistance as the logical consequence of his secularization of the idea of vocation. If one may serve God in secular callings, may not one also resist oppression in areas other than formal worship? It must be regretfully laid at this towering Reformer's door that the great body of German Christendom never protested against Hitler until the doctrine and worship of the church itself were tampered with. Luther's morbid fear of anarchy led him to rate peace higher than justice as the most precious factor in political life: "If one (of either) must yield, then right shall yield to peace and not peace to right." [24]

Calvin, too, ranked peace as of first political importance. But while Luther stresses the *establishment* of the state by God, Calvin stresses its *limitation* by God. This difference in emphasis has been reflected historically in nations dominated respectively by the Lutheran and Calvinist branches of the Reformation. In contrast to Lutheranism's abandonment of secular life to the authority of the state, Calvinism sees the whole of life as informed by a relationship to an authority which transcends the state. No one could have been better qualified to express this than Abraham Kuyper, the great Dutch theologian-statesman of the turn of the century:

> Calvinism is to be praised for having built a dam across [the] absolutistic stream, not by appealing to popular force, nor to the hallucination of human greatness, but by deducing [the] rights and liberties of social life from the same source from which the high authority of government flows, even the absolute sovereignty of God. ... A people therefore which abandons to State Supremacy the right of the family, or a University which abandons to it the rights of science, is just as guilty before God, as a nation which lays its hands upon the rights of the magistrates. And thus the struggle for liber-

ty is not only declared permissible, but is made a duty for each individual in his own sphere.²⁵

Geneva under Calvin was hardly an ideal place in which for individualists to live. He was far from equating liberty with laissez-faire. Yet "freedom means more than half of life," he said in speaking of the bondage of the Israelites in Egypt. And he strongly upheld the view that laws exist to maintain "the right of each individual to his person and his goods." ²⁶

In Calvin, Luther's pessimistic view of man is retained without modification, but it is held in tension with a more thorough-going application of the principle of divine sovereignty. This is why he can take the apparently self-contradictory position that in spite of man's total depravity he still possesses rights by virtue of the image of God. A proper understanding of Calvin's anthropology has long been obscured by a tendency to interpret it in terms of substance rather than relationship. Thus the *imago Dei* is thought of as a thing, and total depravity as a quantitative privation of good. That this interpretation does Calvin an injustice is ably shown by T. F. Torrance of Aberdeen in his carefully documented monograph, *Calvin's Doctrine of Man*. Actually, by total depravity, the Geneva Reformer meant man's total inability to "tend toward a right end," ²⁷ which utterly perverts and vitiates all of his sublime endowments. In this sense, according to Calvin, man has indeed lost the *imago Dei*—the dynamic relationship of continuous conformity to God's will. Nevertheless, while "obliterated" *in* man, the *imago* yet, so to speak, "hangs over" him.²⁸

Because the providence of God continues to maintain order in the world, He keeps alive the distinction between justice and injustice among men, as well as the distinction between men and brutes. This is what Calvin means when he speaks of a "remnant" or "portion" of the *imago* remaining in man. But this is really only an "external image," an "outward semblance" of righteousness.²⁹ As far as saving power is concerned, the image really is obliterated. More important to our topic is the notion that "God does not forego His original intention in regard to the creation of man in His own image, and therefore man's destiny in the image remains in spite of the fact that in himself he is totally depraved." [30] This is brought out with special clarity in Calvin's commentary on Genesis 9:6, "For in the image of God made He man," where the connection with human rights is made explicit:

> Men are indeed unworthy of God's care, if respect be had only to themselves; but since they bear the image of God engraven on them, He deems Himself violated in their person. Thus, although they have nothing of their own by which they obtain the favor of God, He looks upon His own gifts in them, and is thereby excited to love and care for them. This doctrine is to be carefully observed, that no one can be injurious to his brother without wounding God Himself. . . . Should any one object, that this divine image has been obliterated, the solution is easy; first, there yet exists some remnant of it, so that man is possessed of no small dignity; and secondly, the Celestial Creator Himself, however corrupted man may be, still keeps in view the end of His original creation, and according to His example, we ought to consider for what end He created men, and what excellence He has bestowed upon them above the rest of living beings.[31]

Again, in the *Institutes* we read:

> We must not regard the intrinsic merit of men, but must consider the image of God in them, to which we owe all possible honour and love. . . . Say that he is contemptible and worthless; but the Lord shows him to be one whom He has deigned to grace with His own image. Say that you are obliged to him for no services; but God has made him, as it were, His substitute, to whom you acknowledge yourself to be under obligations for numerous and important benefits. Say that he is unworthy of you making the smallest exertion on his account; but the image of God, by which he is recommended to you, deserves your surrender of yourself and all you possess. . . . He has deserved, you will say, a very different treatment from

me. But what has the Lord deserved? Who, when He commands you to forgive men all their offenses against you, certainly intends that they should be charged to Himself. This is the only way of attaining that which is not only difficult, but utterly repugnant to the nature of Man—to love them that hate us, to requite injuries with kindnesses, and to return blessings for curses. We should remember, that we must not reflect on the wickedness of men, but contemplate the divine image in them; which, without concealing and obliterating their faults, by its beauty and dignity allures us to embrace them in the arms of our love.[32]

This latter passage betrays the inferiority in one respect of Calvin to Luther as a social theorist, in that it blurs the distinction between love and justice. Because we revere the image of God in the wicked, we may be obliged, in our purely personal relationships, to requite injuries with kindnesses. But because we revere the image of God in all men, we are more generally obliged to requite evil with justice.[33] As Brunner remarks,

in Calvin . . . the principle of *equitas, équité naturelle,* perpetually merges into the principle of love . . . . The correct idea that on the one hand the order of justice *serves* love, and the *motive* of love includes or gives birth to the just intention, is confused with the other, that justice and love are the same thing.[34]

It may appear strange that the fastidious Calvin should be guilty of imprecision in this matter, especially as compared with Luther, but it should be remembered that the distinction was a cardinal and recurrent theme in Luther's thought. That Calvin did not really differ with him in intent, is seen elsewhere in the *Institutes,* where he justifies the infliction of public retribution upon wrong-doers.[35]

At any rate, the thing to be remembered is that God's ultimate sovereign will is more normative for Calvin's social ethic than is the empirical worthlessness of fallen man. God will not allow His purpose in creation to be thwarted. He has provided in Christ's Atonement the means for the salvation of His elect.* Yet even the elect have no inherent righteousness. They are witnesses to the glory of God. But "the power and the substance lie in the object witnessed to and not in the witness itself." [37] In other words, "the *imago Dei* is interpreted teleologically as above and beyond man in terms of man's destiny which is made known in the Word of God, and in the claim of the divine Will thus revealed upon man's life." [38] As an elect person, comments Troeltsch, "the individual has no value of his own, but as an instrument, to be used for the tasks of the Kingdom of God, his value is immense." [39] Therefore, the elect have rights by virtue of their ultimate destiny, and also by virtue of their special calling to glorify God in this life. Since Calvin, unlike many of his followers, held that God alone can know objectively whom He has elected,[40] rights, in practice, must be extended to everybody—at least everybody not manifestly reprobate.

In contrast to Luther's emphasis upon docile resignation, the Calvinist doctrine of vocation is both fluid and dynamic. The Christian is not to take for granted either the station or the world into which he is born. Assured of his calling and election, he is freed—indeed obligated—to bend all his efforts to the improvement of his station in order to be better able to mold the world into a closer likeness to the Kingdom. "He cannot leave the world alone in all its horror and comfort himself with the thought of a 'finished salvation.' " [41] The building of the Kingdom becomes a peculiarly disciplined and rationalized endeavor which takes the form of labor in the service of impersonal social usefulness.[42] Lutheran irrationalism, inwardness, and sense of immediacy have here

---

*Torrance points out that Calvin's position that God has not let go His original intention in creating man in His own image, and that, therefore, man's destiny in the image remains in spite of total depravity, "is hardly consistent with the doctrine that some men are expressly predestined to damnation." [36]

given way to a cool resolve which does not hesitate to harness the intellect to its purposes, and which prizes concrete efforts over subjective raptures. When this virile and militant outlook is conjoined with the notion that the call to service carries with it a right to freedom in that service, it is no wonder that, as Troeltsch concludes, in inner significance and historical power, the social thrust of Calvinism far outdistances French egalitarian democracy, state socialism, and even proletarian communism.[43]

. . .

Yet despite their historically potent impact, the sociopolitical implications of Calvinist theology have never received really systematic elaboration in terms of the construction of a normative position. Worthy efforts have indeed been made, but one looks in vain for a definitive development of the theory of human rights for which Calvin offered such a firm, incisive starting-point. Our day has witnessed a major revival of Calvinist ideas in the work of the so-called "dialectical" or "Neo-Reformation" theologians. Inasmuch as these theologians, and particularly Brunner and Reinhold Niebuhr, address themselves extensively to social theory, one would expect to discover in their writings the definitive contribution not found elsewhere. It is no disparagement of their many sound and provocative insights to question whether they have provided such a contribution.

Sidney Hook has observed that Niebuhr's social and political views do not stem logically from his theological assumptions.[44] Brunner remained, with some modification, under the influence of the "Social Christianity" of Ragaz, "the Swiss Rauschenbusch," long after he had abandoned the liberal theology from which it stemmed.[45] Their social teachings, where an outgrowth of their mature theological beliefs, are at the same time afflicted with a kind of cynicism which savors more of Luther than of Calvin. From the finitude of human intellect and the corruption of human motivations, both draw despairing judgments as to the possibility of embodying eternal principles of right in human law. While the absolutization of any human system is presumptuous, this should not preclude human efforts to approximate the absolute. The realization of a perfectly just society may be an "impossible possibility," but this does not authorize us to throw up our hands and refuse to undertake the task of rational construction. Niebuhr's cynicism does not lead him to passivity, it is true, but to a sort of relativistic activism critical of all utopian pretensions, which was nonetheless oriented toward Marxist economics at the outset and which has never rid itself of a collectivistic bias. In the case of Brunner the tendency is rather toward the preservation of any status quo within which even a modicum of justice can be realized. This tendency is buttressed by his doctrine of the "orders of creation," a vestigial remnant of Thomist-Lutheran patriarchalism.

Because such disabilities vitiate the social outlook of these perceptive thinkers to whom we must admit in so many ways profound indebtedness, it is imperative that someone venture a fresh elucidation of the social implications of theonomy. I have presumed, while all too keenly conscious of inadequacy, to set my hand to this task in the ensuing chapters. I am fully sensible that what follows is little better than an outline, but present it in the hope that it adumbrates, however sketchily, the true lineaments of a consistently theocentric social ethic which others, better equipped than I, may be prompted to strengthen and to flesh in with detail.*

---

*Despite the fact that this essay is basically the development of an insight found in Calvin, no effort has, of course, been made to stay slavishly within the confines of his thought. I am well aware that he would have taken strong exception to my treatment of several social issues. But, after all, did not even his staunch disciple, John Knox, depart from his teaching concerning the limits of resistance to secular authority? I regard my personal orientation as broadly Calvinistic, but have not hesitated, where appropriate, to draw upon ideas from men as far removed from Calvinism as Herbert Spencer, Rainer Maria Rilke, and Nicholas Berdyaev.

*Part One—The Foundations of Human Rights*

# Axiology: Rights and the Ground of Worth

Let us begin with that which man reveres but does not choose, that which carries as its sign intense and boundless suffering, that which the untutored consciousness proclaims as holy—that is, separate from itself. It cannot be, as Feuerbach thought, a projection of human desires, however lofty, for it constitutes a challenge and a threat to those desires. Let us begin with absolute value, sternly uncompromising in its unconditional demand, yet gracious in the very fact of its self-disclosure. Let us acknowledge it as that to which we must seek to reconcile our ideas of God. Let us acknowledge it, therefore, as God. Let us recognize that it cannot be stated propositionally, that it cannot be defined analytically, and that it cannot be compassed rationally. But let us recognize that *it is*.

There are those whose sophistication will be intolerably affronted by such acknowledgment and recognition. Let us leave them with their sophistication and go our way, wishing them a good deliverance. We cannot tarry in a vain attempt to prove that which can only be experienced. It has other and more pressing claims upon our efforts.

The quest for meaning is itself meaningless except as an endeavor pursued in the service of some value structure. Even the pursuit of knowledge for its own sake rests upon an antecedent value judgment about knowledge. Therefore, if we are to get at the meaning of human rights, our ultimate starting-point must be a discussion of value. Yet, since all reasoning presupposes some judgment of value, we cannot reason about value without commencing with something "given." Such reasoning, if carried far enough, will point beyond itself to the idea of perfection, which reason cannot circumscribe. In Irwin Edman's words,

> Even the most stringent thinking begins with what is precedent to thought; it culminates in what is beyond its operations. At the beginning and the end the thinker knows what he cannot prove; the process of thinking is bounded at both ends by the ineffable.[1]

We need not hesitate to employ the term God to signify the ineffable perfection which bounds the realm of thought. But God cannot be reduced to a logical presupposition or deduction. St. Anselm's famous ontological proof was an attempt to establish God's actual existence as a necessary inference from the idea of perfection. If his critics are correct in their rejection of this method as fallacious, they have merely demonstrated that the finite cannot comprehend the infinite, that the human mind cannot autonomously arrive at the ground and fulfillment of its own activity. Although God's existence may be a necessary idea, only personal encounter with the living Word reveals it to be more than an idea. Faith cannot be rationally coerced: it is, in the final analysis, a gift.

The apprehension of value in a formal sense is, as Kant discerned, a universal innate fact of consciousness, which he identified with duty. Starting with duty, Kant postulated God's existence as an external means of reconciling the dutiful disposition with happiness, the latter being ruled out as a motive for the former, but asserted as requisite to the underlying harmony of the rational and moral universe.[2] In these passages, at least, God appears to be brought in as a sort of after-thought, a logical agent for rendering the good will ultimately productive of felicity. Yet since Kant insisted unequivocally that "nothing in the world—indeed nothing even beyond the world—can possibly be conceived which could be called good without qualification except a good will," [3] and since he would not have been willing to concede that God can be anything less than absolutely good, his own premises give rise to the inference that God should be identified with the good will itself. There are, as a matter of fact, passages in the *Opus Postumum* which suggest that at the end of his life he may have consciously moved toward such an identification, although scholars are in disagreement on this point.[4] In any case, the concept of God as essentially the good will is eminently fruitful regardless of whether or not it was explicitly set forth by Kant, and need not be equated, if the good will be interpreted in a more comprehensive sense than his, with a fundamentally immanentist view of deity. It is also profoundly faithful to the Biblical teaching that the nature of God is best described as love.

The idea of duty implies something more ultimate than itself, in terms of which it exists. If duty is to have any moral significance at all, one must define it as that which value commands. The good will may thus be understood as transcendently self-contained on the divine level, and as reflected on the human level as obedience to the duty of conforming to it for its own sake. Here the obedience of Jesus becomes intelligible as the good will revealing itself dialectically in a movement of unconditional demand and response which fulfills and validates the life of man by raising it above itself. Man transcends creaturehood only as he accepts it in obedience to the demand which absolute value makes upon him, and in his acknowledgment that this very acceptance represents absolute value working in him—that it is truly God who speaks when man sincerely prays: "Not my will but Thine be done." Kant was correct in his assertion that duty predicates freedom; he was also correct in identifying absolute value with the dutiful response, at least for man. If

27

the good will consists in obedience to the claim of value yet is itself identified with value, its human exercise in freedom is a paradox unless value be regarded as basically immanent in man. Thus Kant characteristically speaks of the good will as the disposition of finite rational beings to act in accordance with laws which they prescribe to themselves as expressions of their own rational nature. But faith is not afraid of paradox. And it is only proximately that value can be equated with the dutiful disposition, for it involves a focus which is liberal rather than dutiful, magnanimous rather than punctilious. To define God as ineffable perfection would be sterile were it not for the recognition that perfection, while self-contained, is nonetheless dynamic, revealing itself in a gracious self-disclosure which constitutes at the same time an unlimited claim. It reveals itself in a good will which is both creative and constitutive of value.

Henry Nelson Wieman, whose value theory culminates in an empirical theology, considers it imprecise to attribute personality to absolute value or God, because he mistakenly conceives personality to be something creaturely and relative. Hence, he speaks of God as the impersonal "creative event." Still, he understands that "the mythical symbol of person or personality may be indispensable for the practice of worship and personal devotion to the creative power. . . ." [5] Surely, absolute value cannot be less than conscious, yet how can consciousness be assigned to an event? And why should personality be seen as necessarily creaturely and relative? For our part we do not scruple to say that God is personal, for we affirm Him as creative will, and will is the very core of personality. To say that God is personal is to say that absolute value is dynamically integral, that it transcends the dichotomy between subjectivity and objectivity, universality and particularity, freedom and necessity.

The affirmation that absolute value is dynamically integral indicates that it possesses, together with profound diversity, a simplicity and ultimacy which renders it impervious to analytical definition. Centuries before G. E. Moore decided that good, being a simple and ultimate term, is analytically indefinable, many a mystic had reached essentially the same conclusion. The Council of Nicaea wrestled with the problem of how to retain this insight without abandoning the equally important one that absolute value is inexhaustibly rich and multiform, and that our apprehension of it, although ineffable, impels symbolic description and communication. Thence arose the orthodox symbol of the Trinity, which holds in inexpugnably mysterious tension the simplicity and diversity of God.

Natural reason, through our innate consciousness of duty, tells us that value is worthy of our unconditional loyalty, regardless of prudential considerations. It tells us that the good will requires and incorporates the will to justice. But it does not tell us what the good will is in its quintessence. For the innate consciousness sees absolute value only as refracted by its own self-centeredness as a rival to its own absolute pretensions, and cannot conceive it save under the aspect of judgment and therefore condemnation. Only a supernatural initiative could disclose its heart—could breach the barrier erected by the human ego, and reveal that God is love.

It is only on the human plane that the good will manifests itself as a response elicited by value, although faith will testify that this response does not originate with man. But the initial movement of the dialectic is not one of response to value but of condescension, of self-giving wholly gratuitous and never bestowed as a matter of right upon its object. This is why the good will is so imperfectly represented by the Kantian idea of rational virtue as that which wills evenhanded justice. Kant himself must have been aware of this inadequacy, inasmuch as he allowed a place in his theory for divine forgiveness, despite its inconsistency with the rest of his position.[6] The idea of rigorous and evenhanded justice as asserted by the good will is not in itself imperfect. As we shall later see, it does indeed describe a vital aspect of the good will in its upward and horizontal movements. But it cannot without perversion be equated with the good will in any comprehensive sense.

Strictly speaking, God cannot be positively just to man but only gracious. Justice consists in giving value its due, and there is nothing so valuable in man as to command a debt from God. The relative owes even its existence to the absolute; the absolute owes nothing to the relative. To say that God is just is not to say that He is just to men except in terms of negative retribution, for otherwise He would not be God. To say that God is just is to say that He demands justice of men, horizontally as among themselves, and vertically as toward Himself. His holiness is, in fact, nothing other than His demand for justice toward Himself; it is the refusal of absolute value to share its claim to absolute allegiance with inferior values.

There is another way in which the unlimited association of the good will with the just motive is inadequate. The good will in its gracious and creative dynamism wills not merely justice but also truth and beauty, even as it is itself their apex. Kant, in his characterization of the good will as the rational will, paid tribute to the fundamental unity of truth and justice on the horizontal level, but only indirectly and by implication did he acknowledge that truth, since it transcends the horizontal level, transcends also the principle of universal consistency. The divine self-giving is not bound by universal law: it is its author not its creature. Rules of distributive justice are not germane to it, for it is totally gratuitous and supererogatory.

Since beauty is the direct sensory expression of absolute value in its downward thrust, it is a mode of grace and therefore above law. It prescribes the rules of taste but is not subsumed under them. The aesthetic confrontation is an unconceptualized demand which is not experienced as duty because it carries no horizontal imperative, evoking a spontaneous appreciative response which is complete within itself. Yet at the same time it kindles an impulse to open the self further to its penetration by cultivating disciplined awareness, and this impulse is a manifestation of the voice of duty even if it be not often so conceived. Moreover, the response to beauty has a creative as well as a contemplative side. The sensory expression of transcendence demands imaginative recapitulation, concrete objectification by the hand of man. Art is in this respect an immediate celebration of the divine: the artist knows his work to be a calling, a privilege which is yet an awesome and unsparing obligation. This obligation has no horizontal stratum: the communication of beauty to others is a by-product not the end of the artist's fundamental task. Like the good will, which in it discloses itself to sensibility, beauty is to be venerated solely for its own sake, through creative effort as through contemplation.

The good will, multiform in its revealedness, alone possesses intrinsic worth. In it the potential and the actual are merged in hypostatic union, and it has no end beyond its own existence. Everything else has but contingent worth, depending upon its inherent potential capacity to fulfill its end—complete conformity to its role in the Kingdom of God, the functional hierarchy in which the particularization of the good will finds expression. On this level, then, value may be understood as *entelechia,* the germinal competence of an entity to realize its proper destiny.

We are now ready to attempt a definition of a right. A right is a relationship between value and obligation. It is the claim that value be respected. This claim has an objective pole and a subjective pole. The former is the demand that value be respected in things external to us. The latter is the demand made upon our total being by the potentialities that lie within us. The internal potentiality for the fulfillment of a destined end rightly demands nurture, and renders doubly grave the obligation for positive response toward the realization of that end. This is the teleological meaning of noblesse oblige.

Since rights are dependent upon value, and value is functional, it follows that rights too are functional. Just as value is the inner potentiality of an entity to perform its proper function, so is a right its corresponding claim to external freedom to perform that function. This freedom is the relationship in which respect for value finds expression. If value—the inner potentiality—is lacking, there can be no rights, inasmuch as without it no addition of external freedom can create the necessary capacity.

There is but one exception to the foregoing functional definition of a right. That exception is the absolute right of God. God's value is absolute not relative, intrinsic not instrumental, infinite not finite. Therefore His right is not limited, like that of man, to functional freedom, but incorporates the title to make infinite positive demands. If God had not created or redeemed man, or done anything at all for him, He would still have an absolute claim upon him simply by virtue of what He is in Himself.

Turning from the supra-human to the sub-human level, there is a certain sense in which even inanimate objects may be said to possess rights insofar as they possess value. Something like the rights of inanimate objects is implied in the scriptural mandate to "use the world, as not abusing it." [7]

Inanimate objects have a literal right to protection against wanton spoliation. David G. Ritchie scoffs at the idea of ascribing rights to "pictures or stones . . . because a work of art or some ancient monument is protected by law from injury," [8] but he gives no reasons for the alleged absurdity of such ascription. The shelling of the Parthenon, the bombardment of Monte Cassino— these were crimes not alone against humanity but against the things themselves, against priceless concretions of objective worth. It is true that inanimate things derive their value from a relationship which they bear to man, but it is not a value which man confers subjectively upon them. It is man, rather, who participates in the realm of values as he takes his place in the objective structure of relationships which all things have to one another ideally in terms of the cosmic hierarchy of ends.

"It is possible to see in a still life by Cézanne, an animal picture by Marc, and a landscape by Schmidt-Rotluff, the direct revelation of an absolute reality in these relative things." So speaks Paul Tillich. "The world-import experience in the artist's religious ecstasy shines through the things; they have become 'holy' objects." [9]

To anyone in whom the torture of a cat or the flogging of a horse arouses indignation that goes deeper than aesthetic or emotional repugnance, there is nothing ludicrous in the assertion that animals have rights. It is the sense of justice which is outraged by such acts. Humane treatment of animals is clearly enjoined by Scripture in numerous passages found mainly in the Book of Deuteronomy. One of these (Deuteronomy 25:4) seems to imply that the ox has a *right* to a portion of the grain he has helped tread out.

But to respect the rights of animals does not by any means require that one must embrace vegetarianism or become an anti-vivisectionist. Their rights proceed from their functions in the telic hierarchy, and it is not presumptuous to assume on Biblical authority that these functions are subordinate to those of man.[10] Here again the rule applies: "to use as not to abuse." To abuse a creature is not only to use it cruelly but to use it for unworthy ends. To bob the tail of a dog is a clearer violation of animal rights than to slaughter a hog; to breed bulls for the ring a clearer violation than to dissect guinea pigs. However, since the topic of this book is *human* rights, I shall not insist upon pressing this argument any further. Instead, it is now fitting that we should examine the nature of man in the light of the distinctive end for which he was created.

## Chapter Two

# Teleology: The Vocation of Man

Speculation as to the "why" of human existence receives its most profound and comprehensive answer in the familiar words of the Westminster Shorter Catechism: "to glorify God and enjoy Him forever." This seemingly simple statement, devoid of meaning to the positivist, is for the believer an inexhaustible fount of spiritual illumination which irradiates and clarifies in principle the whole of life. For "the natural man receiveth not the things of the Spirit of God, for they are foolishness unto him, neither can he know them, because they are spiritually discerned." [1] But the man of faith affirms with Augustine and Anselm, "I believe [in order] that I may know," echoing in his heart the declaration of the Psalmist: "With thee is the fountain of life, and in thy light do we see light." [2] Such belief, of course, is not a matter of servile submission to external authority (as some passages in Augustine and Anselm might suggest), but a matter of free, experiential loyalty.[3] The catechetical definition is, however, an abstract one, and can be made to yield specific content only as interpreted by a creatively devout imagination drawing upon insights from whatever sources, be they "sacred" or "secular," through which the vivifying Spirit of Truth imparts its witness. Using this method, I have been led to approach the formal definition

*34*

from four angles, each of which represents a different, yet integrally related, dimension of its content. These dimensions (which posit each other at the highest level of development) I shall call respectively, for want of better terminology, mystical union, creative perception, psychological integration, and social communion. Let us examine each of these in turn.

• • •

Mystical union is a term which I employ with hesitation, as it has an exotic sound, suggestive of pantheism. As I use it, however, it does not signify impersonal absorption or some beatific state of consciousness to which man can ascend through the use of esoteric spiritual techniques. It refers to that dimension of man's purpose voiced by Jesus in the Sermon on the Mount, when He said: "You must be perfect, even as your heavenly Father is perfect." [4] This is a charge to unity of moral will with God. If one takes seriously the Johannine statement that God is love, one perceives that such a moral union constitutes also a substantial union. Man becomes truly human only as he becomes divine. As Nicholas Berdyaev tells us, "the secret of Christianity is the secret of God-manhood," [5] and it is to the credit of the Eastern Church, of which he was such a distinguished representative, that it preserved and emphasized this important scriptural concept while the West was largely preoccupied with theological notions of a forensic character.

> Theosis makes man divine, inducts him into the divine life, while at the same time it preserves his human nature. Thus instead of the human personality being annihilated, it is changed into the likeness of God and the divine Trinity.[6]

Such is the creation's fundamental goal, and the ontological import of that single-hearted obedience to the Father's will so matchlessly portrayed by the archetypal God-man, Jesus Christ. In the great allegorical discourse on the

*35*

True Vine, the intimate connection of theosis, both with the glorification and with the enjoyment of God, finds striking expression:

> Abide in me, and I in you. As the branch cannot bear fruit by itself, unless it abides in the vine, neither can you, unless you abide in me. . . . By this the father is glorified, that you bear much fruit, and so prove to be my disciples. . . . These things I have spoken to you, that my joy may be with you, and that your joy may be full.[7]

Moral or essential unity with God is not antithetical to creaturehood; indeed, as Jesus demonstrated in His human role, it is inseparable from the positive acceptance of existence in meaningful dependence and subordination. It is the very opposite of titanism—the urge to possess God's attributes as a means of self-exaltation. According to the Genesis account the primeval disobedience consisted in precisely this. When man responded to the serpent's lure—"Eat of this fruit and ye shall be as gods" (i.e., possessing the attributes without the essence of deity), he set his will against the will of his Creator, and destroyed his own potentiality for theandric being. He preferred the "accidents" to the "substance" of divinity. Wisdom (symbolized by the Tree of Knowledge of Good and Evil), immortality (symbolized by the Tree of Life), and power (symbolized in its false semblance by the Tower of Babel)—all these are perverted and ultimately unreal apart from love, apart from unity of moral will with God. On the other hand, if such moral unity obtains, man transcends finitude. He becomes immortal, a partaker in eternal life.[8] He realizes that the divine wisdom and power exist to serve the Will in which his own will rests. This realization causes him to accept affirmatively his external, empirical limitations, for he sees them as of no consequence once he has been freed from the internal limitations imposed by "fallen" consciousness or "objectification," that is to say, by the estrangement of the ego from its Source. This is why the Apostle Paul could write:

> I am sure that neither death, nor life, nor angels, nor principalities, nor powers, nor things present, nor things to come, nor height, nor depth, nor anything else in all creation, will be able to separate us from the love of God in Jesus Christ our Lord.[9]

. . . . . . . . . . . . . . . . . . . . . . . . . . .

> Though our outer nature is wasting away, our inner nature is being replaced every day . . . because we look not to the things that are seen but to the things that are unseen; for the things that are seen are transient, but the things that are unseen are eternal.[10]

• • •

In the words of Bernard Eugene Meland, "God has created human beings to become structures of consciousness that will be creators and carriers of spirit, and in this, to glorify Him. . . ." [11] Thus creative perception is apprehended as a dimension of man's purpose.

Full humanity demands a disciplined sensitivity and a heightening of appreciative awareness. It demands the ability, as William Blake expressed it,

> To see the world in a grain of sand,
> and a heaven in a wild flower:
>
> [To] hold infinity in the palm of your hand,
> and eternity in an hour.

It demands the cultivation of the imagination, and of the sense of form. It demands the sustained experience of awe and wonder. It demands the perception of quality, and its triumph within the consciousness over undifferentiated mass and number. It demands an effort of the intellect which is strenuous and at the same time humble. It demands the rational-intuitive assimilation of that which lies behind the superficial sphere of fact. In a remarkable letter to his Polish translator, the poet Rilke called this "the task of transformation":

> Nature, the things we move about among and use, are provisional and perishable; but, so long as we are here, they are OUR possession and our friendship, sharers in our trouble and gladness, just as they have been the con-

fidants of our ancestors. Therefore, not only must all
that is here not be corrupted or degraded, but just
because of that very provisionality they share with us,
all these appearances and things should be comprehended by us in a most fervent understanding, and
transformed. Transformed? Yes, for our task is to stamp
this provisional, perishing earth into ourselves so deeply,
so painfully and passionately, that its being may arise
again, "invisibly," in us.[12]

Man was created to create, to think God's thoughts
after Him, to actualize relative values and to participate
in absolute value. He was meant to enter in this way into
the dynamic life of the Logos. Rilke celebrates one aspect
of this process—the spiritualization of the external world
of objects. Berdyaev celebrates its other aspect—the creative dialectic of the shared spiritual life between subjects, i.e., imaginative inter-personal communion. This,
too, is an aesthetic and an intellectual calling, although
it is much more.[13] Berdyaev even goes so far as to say that
it is necessary to the enrichment of God's inward being:
"God has need of man, of his creative response to the
divine summons." [14] This we cannot accept, for to do so
would be to minimize God's condescension, and to make
His altruism something less than perfect. God wills man's
creative response, not for His own sake but for the sake of
man. Absolute value (i.e., God) is by definition self-
contained, and its realization is not dependent upon anything external to itself. Man's participation in it adds
nothing to it. It is true that relative values depend for
their actualization upon man's response, but they can
obviously add nothing to that which is intrinsically complete.* Why should Deity, self-contained and perfect, will
the communion of another being? Why does God suffer
in the absence of something which can benefit Him not
at all? To ask such questions is to betray the corruption

---

*"The divine love is not the longing of a needy soul for fulfillment—
that is *eros*, not *agapē*. The divine love is the welling up of the Perfect.
It is the love of the triune God which needs no other in order to love
because in Himself He is all-sufficient love" (Emil Brunner, *Man in
Revolt*, trans. Olive Wyon, New York: Scribners, 1939, p. 493).

of human nature, which apprehends love only as a valuation based upon the loved one's real or fancied utility as a means of gratifying the self. From where man stands, agapē can be known only as a benignant paradox, as the inscrutable but providential mystery which lies at the very heart and center of creation.

• • •

The close bearing of creative perception upon the psychological dimension of man's purpose comes out clearly in Walter Lippmann's description of maturity, which leads us, without passing beyond the bounds of sober analysis, to the threshold of a delineation of the noetic level of awareness:

> The understanding creates a new environment. The more subtle and discriminating, the more informed and sympathetic the understanding is, the more complex and yet ordered do the things about us become. To most of us, as Mr. Santayana once said, music is a pleasant noise which produces a drowsy revery relieved by nervous thrills. But the trained musician hears what we do not hear at all; he hears the form, the structure, the pattern, and the significance of an ideal world. A naturalist out of doors perceives a whole universe of related life which the rest of us do not even see. A world which is ordinarily unseen has become visible through the understanding. When the mind has fetched it out of the flux of dumb sensations, defined and fixed it, this unseen world becomes more real than the dumb sensations it supplants. When the understanding is at work, it is as if circumstance had ceased to mutter strange sounds and had begun to speak our language. When experience is understood, it is no longer what it is wholly to the infant, very largely to youth, and in great measure to most men, a succession of desirable objects at which they instinctively grasp, interspersed with undesirable ones from which they instinctively shrink. If objects are seen in their context, in the light of their origin and destiny, with sympathy for their own logic and their own purposes, they become interesting in themselves, and are no longer blind stimuli to pleasant and unpleasant sensations....
>
> In place of a world, where like children we are minis-

tered to by a solicitous mother, the understanding introduces us into a world where delight is reserved for those who can appreciate the meaning and purpose of things outside themselves, and can make these meanings and purposes their own.[15]

Noesis, the fulness of creative perception, involves not merely a heightening but also an integration of the consciousness. Maurice Nicoll speaks to this point from the vantage station of a physician and psychiatrist:

> The end of man is the attainment of this further state of himself. All the different parts of him, like the separate parts of a machine, are not understandable or relatable, unless the final aim and meaning of the whole is grasped. Otherwise, one investigator takes hold of one part, another another part, and in each case gives the significance of the whole to the part, so that only contradiction and, what is worse, a malinterpretation of man, result.[16]

. . . . . . . . . . . . . . . . . . . . . . . . . .

> If we could see all the relations and affinities that an object has, simultaneously, instead of as a confused collection of separately noticed properties, which often seem to be contradictory, we would be on the *noetic* level of conscious experience. . . . The separate sensible properties of the object would be merged into its *total significance*. It would be seen as an expression of the universe, so that while nothing that our senses told us of it would be lost sight of or wrong, it would be invested with a meaning that transcended all sensible perception and would become a manifestation of "intelligible form" or idea.[17]

In this kind of consciousness, time is overcome. Mere duration gives way to a quality of experience in which the moment comprehends within itself the fulness of reality— the *pleroma*. This is eternal life. To be born "from above" is to know life as a limpid crystal which reveals concurrently every individual atom equally in its superlative distinctiveness and in its relation to the aggregate, every individual instant equally in its radical unrepeatability and in its universal reference.

Noesis should not be construed as something separate and apart from unity of moral will with God. In their ultimate, supreme expression, Truth, Beauty, and Goodness are an indivisible whole, and noesis brings an existential apprehension of this fact. It is not to be denied that in the empirical life of individuals the rational, aesthetic, and volitional faculties may exhibit varying respective stages of development from one person to the next, but this merely testifies to the fragmented and dislocated character of phenomenal existence. "Natural" creativity can, of course, be egoistic and demonic, and "natural" love is often narrow and uninformed, but these are pathetically distorted counterfeits of authentic creativity and love. Just as, on the one hand, real creativity, the hallmark of what is genuinely aesthetic and intellectual, always involves an effort of the will, so real love, the paramount vocation of the will, always involves creativity.

For our purposes, personality may be defined ideally as consciousness which combines maximal depth and richness of content with perfection of form or integration. It is fully realized only by God, and thus the experience of moral unity with Him is man's only hope for personal integration at the highest level. The centrality of agapē as its fundamental unifying principle is pointed up by Lewis Mumford's remark that to be "capable of loving and ready to receive love, is the paramount problem of integration; indeed the key to salvation." [18]

Man's tendency is toward pseudo-integration. This may take the form of the superficial unification which occurs when the ego crystallizes around some value which is less than all-embracing. Such superficial unification may be termed "psychological abortion." The self is integrated prematurely—before it attains to full depth and richness of content. The result is the destruction of creative tension, and the complacently truncated psyche atrophies and finally disintegrates.[19] Pseudo-integration may also take the form of the distorted unification which occurs when the ego crystallizes around some facet of itself. This facet is usually projected onto an external object which then becomes an idol. This leads to "objectification," the creation of a false and spellbound world. The individual becomes a slave of his distorted imagination.[20]

The two types of pseudo-integration complement one another. Although distorted unification may take place with relatively rich psychological content, it always presupposes a personality abortion at some point. Although superficial unification may be relatively well-oriented as far as it goes, it always presupposes a personality distortion at some point. In the former case, warping inevitably produces a limited perspective. In the latter case, limitation inevitably produces a warped perspective. Only a transcendent referent, the will of God, can give man a true perspective which enables him to see life clearly and to see it whole. Only such a referent can allow for growth, for the painful process of creative tension without which genuine personal integration is impossible. This is why "life adjustment" and "positive thinking" are dangerously inadequate norms for integration. This is why the lives of the greater religious geniuses—Paul, Augustine, Luther, Kierkegaard, Dostoyevski—exhibit a dynamic and often violent inner dialectic of suffering and struggle, which contrasts vividly with the placid equipoise so frequently regarded as the badge of saintliness. The "crucifixion of the old Adam" means a turning away of the ego from itself and its projections to a trans-historical and supra-mundane Good which shatters complacency by virtue of its awesome height.[21]

• • •

Personal integration cannot be severed from the social dimension of man's end, any more than it can be severed from moral unity with God or from noetic consciousness. Inter-personal relationships compose the setting in which God reveals Himself as love.[22] Spiritual growth comes in large measure through shared experience. No one attains fulfillment in a vacuum: self-realization, if authentic, is always manifested by a redemptive concern for others. It is in every instance marked by a giving of the self to another—ultimately to God, proximately to the neighbor. ". . . This realization is invariably accompanied by self-limitation, a free subordination of the self to the supra-personal, the creation of supra-personal values, the escape from self and the penetration of other selves." [23] What Rollo May says about erotic love is even more apposite to the outreach of a spirit kindled by agapē: "As in creative ecstasy, it is that moment of self-realization when one temporality overleaps the barrier between one identity and another. It is a giving of the self and a finding of the self at once." [24]

Theosis is not a matter of absorption into transcendence: it has a horizontal thrust. Noesis is not exhausted by contemplation: it culminates in action. Personal integration is not characterized by a turning in upon the self: it feeds upon communion with others.

> For man, who is involved in the unities and harmonies of nature but who also transcends them in his freedom, there can be no principle of harmony short of the love in which free personality is united in freedom with other persons.[25]

The Kingdom of God is the social dimension of the will of God for man.* It exists germinally wherever *koinonia* exists—the sharing of the gifts of the spirit. This corporate experience of free, noumenal communion of men responding to agapē, has been expressed within the Russian

---

*The validity of this statement does not hinge upon the question of whether or not Jesus thought of the Kingdom in primarily eschatological terms. It is the "reign" and the "realm" of God in the lives of men, and rests upon their acknowledgment of Him as Lord of all life. (See George F. Thomas, *Christian Ethics and Moral Philosophy*, New York: Scribners, 1955, p. 18 ff.) As Thomas says, those who enter it "constitute a community of those who serve God." Although it "is to come by divine intervention and cannot be 'built' by men . . . men must decide for themselves here and now whether, with God's help, they will meet its conditions and therefore will reap its fruits" (Ibid., p. 25).

Orthodox Church by the term, *sobornost,* which has no precise equivalent in English. Its meaning is vulgarized and rendered insipid by the translation, "togetherness," so popular of late in liberal pietistic circles. It has nothing to do with any kind of exoteric collectivity: it is the antithesis of communal life imposed from without. It certainly is not to be equated with the sentimental dissolution of distinctions beneath a roseate mist of cheap and meaningless fraternity. To the euphoric vision of One Big Happy Family, awash in a sea of pink lemonade called "love," or holding hands in mindless dance around a maypole labelled "Jesus," must be opposed as a corrective the idea of the comradeship of battle, wherein those called to serve find through their common sacrifice and hazard a shared presence which binds them together by lifting them beyond themselves.

# Anthropology: The Nature of Empirical Man

It should not require elaborate demonstration to establish that empirical man does not, in fact, begin to measure up to the grand four-fold vocation just delineated. Indeed, it is just his tentative god-likeness which is the occasion for his invariable rebellion and consequent loss of his divine potential. To equate original sin, as does Lecomte du Noüy, with "the survival in man of the ancestral memories" of prehistoric bestiality, is to fail to realize that sin does not have its seat in the animal but in the spiritual side of human nature.[1] "Man," says Reinhold Niebuhr, "is a finite spirit, lacking identity with the whole, but yet a spirit capable in some sense of envisaging the whole, so that he easily commits the error of imagining himself the whole which he envisages." [2] But this "error" is not merely a matter of ignorance; it contains an element of conscious perversity. Standing in the vertiginous juncture of freedom and finitude, man reacts to the anxiety concomitant to his situation by attempting either to deny the contingent character of his existence (in pride and self-love) or to escape from his freedom (in sensuality).[3] It matters little whether this universal fact be interpreted as the hereditary issue of an historical event, or as a repeated experience in the life of Everyman. It is an inescapable part of the data of human existence. This does not mean, however, that rebellion is inevitable; it does not belong to man's essential nature, and is not outside the realm of his responsibility. "Sin is natural for man in the sense that it is universal but not in the sense that it is necessary." [4]*

For many, the central problem of theodicy is how to reconcile God's goodness and omnipotence with His creation of a being capable of sin. Yet such initial capability is prerequisite to man's ultimate perfection, for it is by definition impossible that a free moral agent be created perfect; perfection in this context demands a voluntary effort of the will. An animal or an inanimate object can be created perfect, but man, because he is man and not an animal or an inanimate object, can only be created with a potentiality for perfection. Human perfection must be willed creatively by man; if it were merely created it would not be perfection.

> Thus man's distinctive endowment . . . namely, the fact that he has been made in the image of God, is the presupposition of sin. Sin itself is a manifestation of the image of God in man; only he who has been created in the image of God can sin, and in his sin he shows the "supernatural," spirit-Power, a power not of this world, which issues from the primal image of God. Even where he commits sin man shows his greatness and his superiority. No animal is able to sin, for it is unable to rebel against its destiny, against the form in which it has been created; it has not the power of decision. The Creator has given this dangerous power to His last and highest earthly creature, since He created him not simply *through* His Word, but *in* His Word, and therefore responsible. And it is this very distinctiveness which becomes a temptation to man. The copy wants to be the model itself, the one who ought to answer wishes to be the "word itself," the planet wants to be the sun, a star in its own light. Man "can" do this, thanks to the gift of

---

*Carl F. H. Henry holds that the doctrine of a historical fall is necessary to safeguard against the assumption that sin is inevitable. However, his reasoning on this point is not clear. See his *Christian Personal Ethics* (Grand Rapids: Eerdmans, 1957), p. 182.

the Creator. But if and when he does so, he destroys the possibility of doing what he could have done.[5]

That man (Adam) in his freedom seeks to usurp the divine suzerainty and choose a false autonomy, is an impenetrable mystery to which the Bible gives no clue, and which bears no analogy to anything else in human experience. "Whoever seeks to explain sin, or believes that he can, makes of sin a fate and abolishes the act. The biblical concept of sin is that it is an irrational deed." [6] Apart from the love whereby the redeemed respond to justifying grace, initial sin may be understood as perhaps the only absolutely free act we ever commit, for it is the only act which is wholly independent of causality. Temptation is its precondition but not its cause.

> Behold the infant, helpless in cradle and
> Righteous still, yet already there is
> Dread in his dreams at the deed of which
> He knows nothing but knows he can do,
> The gulf before him with guilt beyond,
> Whatever that is, whatever why,
> Forbids his bound; till that ban tempts him;
> He jumps and is judged: he joins mankind,
> The fallen families, freedom lost,
> Love become Law.[7]

From that point on we are enmeshed in the pattern of our first rebellion. We cannot extricate ourselves. Egocentricity becomes ingrained and controlling, and our whole lives are dominated by the lust for self-assertion. This lust manifests itself in various and subtle forms. It may even appear to be the reverse of what it really is, as "religiousness," or as a striving after self-abnegation. The Buddhist monk who labors for the obliteration of his ego may be just as much an egoist at bottom as Napoleon, for his motivation is a selfish one: emancipation from the wheel of *karma*. And the zealot who submerges his personality in the corporate being of race, state, or class, may do so because only thus is he able to gratify, vicariously as it were, his desire to magnify himself.

As the late Archbishop Temple declared, "from the beginning I put myself in God's place. This is my original sin. I was doing it before I could speak, and every one else has been doing it from early infancy." [8] This event is in a category by itself; it is absolutely *sui generis,* determined neither by logic nor by chance. Because of its uniqueness, we have no criterion for assuming that the calculus of probabilities applies to it. The very radicalness of its indeterminism renders fatuous the question of why, if not determined, "original" sin is universal.

Theosis is an offense to empirical man. Instead of seeking perfect moral unity with God, in his delusion he credits himself with the divine attributes of power, wisdom, and immortality, imagining that because of his freedom to reject God he can henceforth live autonomously. Augustine traces "the slippery motion of falling away" from the good to a "perverse desire for the likeness of God" independently possessed. For the likeness of God "is not preserved except it be in relation to Him by whom it is impressed." [9] Even thus estranged, man yet retains a sense of "the holy," of something numenous outside himself. And this latent apprehension may become more concrete as he becomes increasingly aware that his pretensions clash with reality. He then establishes a new relationship with God, but it is an external and juridical relationship. God has become to him an alien Power which will break him if not placated. So, with the selfish locus of his will unaltered, man engages in a kind of worship which is really magic—a frantic effort to avert doom by wheedling and bribing an Enemy too potent to be ignored. In the highest stages of natural religion, magic gives way to legalism. Man realizes that he ought to love God.

> The task of his life is now the hopeless one of squaring the circle; he ought to do the Good willingly, which, as a duty, cannot be done willingly at all. The Good which can only be done in the natural spirit of love has now become a legalistic demand.[10]

For the locus of his will is still himself. His "devotion to every transcendent value is corrupted by the effort to insert the interests of the self into that value." [11] He cannot sincerely love God because in his initial rebellion he cut himself off from the Source of love.

> If, however, he cannot love—love as one loves in God— then he can no longer fulfil the meaning of his life, that which gives to his life its genuinely human character. He can no longer fulfil the divine meaning of his life, not only in part but not at all; and not only for a time, until he has regained it, but never again: the connexion with God once broken cannot be reunited; the love of God which has been lost cannot be regained.[12]

We could never repent in proportion to our sin, even if present repentance were able to cancel out previous guilt, which it cannot. The result of this is death: permanent estrangement from the Foundation and eternal import of existence, bondage to the meaningless and the ephemeral.

The Fall is essentially a mystical category, but man's loss of the theandric potential carries with it implications for all the dimensions of his purpose. His aesthetic and intellectual proclivities, severed from their proper end, become sources of titanism; his creativity, distorted and perverse.[13] Imagination and reason unite in the production of idols. Instead of attaining to noetic consciousness, the psyche stagnates in warped and limited states of pseudo-integration.[14] By placing itself and its projections in the center of reality, it becomes incapable of true perspective; life is seen as if reflected in the hobgoblin's baneful mirror of Hans Christian Andersen's tale, in which "the most beautiful landscapes looked like boiled spinach." By virtue of its blind insistence upon autonomy, the self ceases to be self-determined and falls prey to the malevolent determinisms emphasized by Marx and Freud.[15] As Reinhold Niebuhr says, injustice is the social dimension of sin. "The ego which falsely makes itself the centre of existence in its pride and will-to-power inevitably subordinates other life to its will and thus does injustice to other life." [16] And this is not simply a predicament of isolated individuals. Josiah Royce, in *The Problem of Christianity*, showed how the very process of socialization arouses our self-will.

> The natural community is, in its united collective will.
> a community of *sin*. Its state is made, by its vast powers,
> worse than that of the individual. But it trains the individual to be as great a sinner as his powers permit.[17]

The recognition that sin is inextricably embedded in the texture of social institutions need not lead us to embrace that maudlin and illogical interpretation of corporate guilt which has achieved such currency in the wake of the Kennedy assassinations and that of Martin Luther King. There is, in the Christian doctrine of sin, no warrant for the incantation "We are all guilty" which seems to rise reflexively from pulpits whenever some shocking act occurs which has broad social impact. It is true that all men are sinners, but not all sinners are guilty of the same specific sins. If it is a sin to have been less than an enthusiastic admirer of John and Robert Kennedy or of King, I willingly intone my *mea culpa*. But I repudiate the suggestion that I, or any significant number of Americans, had anything to do, even indirectly or subjectively, with the tragic events of Dallas, Los Angeles, and Memphis, any more than we had anything to do with Edward Kennedy's tragic accident on Chappaquiddick Island, or with the untimely swimming pool drowning of King's brother. The Wesleyan dictum that sin is "the willing transgression of a known law" may not be adequate as a comprehensive definition, but it does correctly state the nature of sin in its particularity. To ask me to acknowledge guilt for acts with which I had no sympathy and not even the most remote connection is to invite me to place my guilt for acts for which I really am responsible on the same fictitious plane, and thus to dilute and cheapen the idea of guilt itself. If we look into our hearts, we can all find plenty of authentic reasons for repentance, without having to indulge in orgies of self-accusatory bathos over transgressions for which the blame lies elsewhere.

Another point of clarification must be made with respect to the meaning of guilt. When the conditions of our social situation force us into choices which involve evil but which are still the best possibilities open to us, these choices are, in context, good.[18] Reinhold Niebuhr is right when he says that we must not accept complacently the moral limitations imposed upon us by the social structures under which we live, but he is wrong when he ascribes guilt to actions which are derived from the necessities of time and place.[19] Moral guilt is a category which applies to motivation, not to the objective evil in actions shaped by factors external to the motive of the agent. To assert the doctrine of total depravity is not to deny that many of our choices, regardless of their outcome, stem from the disposition to do right, and are therefore morally unimpeachable. It is to assert, rather, that, however much it may influence particular decisions, this disposition does not constitute the ruling focus of our lives— lives which are totally corrupted by self-will as to the *direction* in which they tend.

• • •

It will be remembered that in our analysis of rights and the ground of worth, worth was defined as the inner capacity of an entity to fulfill its proper end, and a right as its corresponding external freedom to do so. An examination of empirical man in the light of his end reveals that he is both actually and potentially incapable of fulfilling it in any of its dimensions. Through sin he has rendered himself unable to be united with the divine Will, unable to translate the visible into the invisible without distortion, unable really to become a person, and unable to participate in the Kingdom.

It is true that fallen man still possesses such remnants of the image of God as enable him to distinguish in a general way between right and wrong, and to know that he is obligated to do the right. He is able even to perform individual acts of virtue. But this is not the issue; the issue is that he is no longer able to fulfill his end, no longer able to orient his total life and being toward that Good to the existence of which his conscience witnesses.[20] His radical estrangement from the Source of worth not only divests him of actual but also of potential value, since of his own initiative he can never overcome his alienation. He possesses no independent worth and has cut himself off from the Source of worth; hence, since rights are correlative to worth, we must conclude that, strictly speaking, man has no rights.* But this is to reckon without God's unfathomable grace.

*Unless rights be defined as nothing but pragmatic fictions to be accepted and modified at will, a point of view which leads to nihilism. Apart from God, rights are meaningless and cannot be sustained even from a contractual standpoint between creatures, for they are without ultimate ground. (See Nicolas Berdyaev, *Freedom and the Spirit,* trans. Oliver Fielding Clarke, New York: Scribners, 1935, passim.) "Enlightened self-interest" does not provide such a ground, for it has no teleological content.

## Chapter Four

# Soteriology: The Social Significance of the Atonement

For my thoughts are not your thoughts, neither are your ways my ways, says the Lord. For as the heavens are higher than the earth, so are my ways higher than your ways and my thoughts higher than your thoughts.[1]

I am God and not man, the Holy One in your midst, and I will not come to destroy.[2]

These amazing words are an affirmation of God's transcendent freedom. As Brunner tells us, "it is not a logical necessity to God to forgive," and "there are no human conditions in which we have the right to expect that God will forgive us as a matter of course." [3] But because He is free He is able to forgive. He is not bound by iron gyves of cause and effect. "The wages of sin is death," and as far as anything man can do about it is concerned, this statement has all the rigid finality of karmic law. Yet what is impossible for man is not impossible for his Creator, hence the statement has a sequel: "but the gift of God is eternal life through Jesus Christ our Lord." [4]

When we say that God is above law and free, we do not mean that He abrogates law or sets it aside, for that would be a denial of His faithfulness and His consistency. What we mean, rather, is that He has within Himself boundless resources for dealing with the irrefrangible sequence of sin and retribution, stratagems of grace which overcome the law without annulling it. His holiness demands that sin be taken seriously. In the words of Athanasius "it was unthinkable that God, the Father of Truth, should go back upon His word regarding death in order to ensure our continued existence." [5] His wrath, which stems inexorably from what Brunner aptly calls "the infinite divine self-respect without which His love would not be divine love but sentimentality," [6] is the expression of his inability to regard sin as if it did not matter. But wrath is not His essence; it is not the ultimate category of deity. If "God is not mocked," neither is His purpose thwarted, and an ultimate reign of wrath would not comport with the realization of His unconditional will for communion with man. This is not the place to elaborate a detailed soteriology; furthermore, it would be dangerously brash to try to lay down apodictically the intricacies of the economy of grace. The meaning of the Atonement is in its fullness ineffable. Still, this much can be said: the Cross which reconciles man to God reconciles at the same time God's justice to God's love. This is something man could never do. God alone could do it—but at what a price! The divine sacrifice is the immeasurable stratagem which makes the divine forgiveness possible without negating the divine holiness. Any effort to spell this out in literal terms is likely to lead to notions of a rationalistic and artificial character. Let us be content to be grateful for something which transcends analysis, humbly and joyfully affirming the incomprehensible fact that God in His graciousness at infinite cost to Himself takes the initiative in healing the breach created by the willfulness of man.

It is a curious phenomenon that, so far as I have been able to discover, no Christian ethicist, regardless of how orthodox or evangelical, has sought the ground of human rights objectively and specifically in the Atonement,*

---

*Walter Rauschenbusch's *A Theology for the Social Gospel* (New York: Abingdon Press, 1945) contains a chapter entitled "The Social Gospel and the Atonement," but his interpretation of the Atonement is a mere moral influence theory.

although such a ground was certainly implied by Calvin.* Paul Ramsey seems to move in that direction when he says that

> motivation for valuing human personality is to be derived neither from the created nature of man nor indirectly by implication from man's created capacity for responsive service of God. . . . Personality and its rights are in Christian ethics read, as it were, backward from Christ into man.[7]

We are to attribute worth to the neighbor because Christ does so. But nothing is said about the "transaction" which makes this valuation possible. Carl F. H. Henry predicates the whole of Christian ethics on the Atonement, which, as a conservative evangelical, he interprets forensically, but he does not specifically relate this to the question of rights. Instead he speaks of claims which all men have "because they share a common human nature in creation," and because they are "bearers of the imago Dei." [8] Albert C. Knudson is one of many others who emphasize the *imago Dei* as the source of human worth. "The object of true love must have personal worth. . . . It was God in men, in oneself and in others that gave to them their moral worth and made them proper objects of Christian love." [9] (Knudson evidently identifies Christian love with eros rather than agapē.) As for John C. Bennett, he not only neglects to base human rights on the Atonement, but explicitly refuses to do so, asserting that "no doctrine of the incarnation and no theory of redemption can take the place of the historical Jesus as the source of goals and dynamic for social change." [10] According to Bennett "the worth of persons which is a basic assumption of [Jesus'] ethic is known from God's love for them." [11] This is, of course, a gross humanistic denial of the very kernel of the gospel. God does not love persons because they have worth but in spite of their lack of worth. It will be recalled that all three of the synoptic

---

*See my Prolegomena, pp. 1–22.

gospels report Jesus as having said: "No one is good but God alone." [12] The nature of agapē is better understood by George F. Thomas, who rightly remarks that "God's love is not measured out according to the value of the person loved, as human love is; rather, God is the Creator and His love is *creative* of worth." [13] However, he goes on to say that the sinner has some worth as a creature made in the image of God, and that God's love is creative, "not in the sense that it gives value to a being that is wholly without value, but that it brings to fulfillment possibilities of value that were present but frustrated." [14] Yet this does not make sense according to our definition of worth as the inner capacity of a thing to fulfill its end, for from the human standpoint this capacity is so thoroughly and completely frustrated as to not exist even as a possibility. As Ramsey makes clear,[15] the image of God is not something inherent in the substantial form of human nature but is to be understood as a relationship within which man stands whenever like a mirror he obediently reflects God's will.

> Man and God do not resemble each other directly, but conversely; only when God has infinitely become the eternal and omnipresent object of worship, and man always a worshipper, do they resemble one another.[16]

This is the relationship in which we were created, but all that now remains of it outside the revelation of God's grace in Christ, is the general apprehension of a Good without which there could be no consciousness of sin. The innocent and spontaneous love of God has given place to the knowledge of good and evil, and no man has ever been redeemed by merely knowing the difference between right and wrong.[17]

Any "kataphatic" explanation of the vicarious role of Christ is bound to be misleading, since it issues in fruitless speculation as to how one individual can atone for another's guilt and how one individual's righteousness can be imputed to another. We should not be so concerned with the literal mechanics of His work of substitu-

tion that we lose sight of its significance as dramatic myth
expressive of a truth which can only be comprehended
symbolically, not reduced to strictly rational formulation.[18] The Atonement is a divine act which is not literally analogous to anything in human experience. It is a
mistake to try to read it as a strict expression of the
categories of human legal justice. If not pressed too far,
such categories are, however, metaphorically helpful, and
when thrown out completely—as, for example, by Rauschenbusch[19]—the doctrine becomes thin and sentimental. The important thing is that God does impute to
sinful man a value not inherent in him, namely, the
"righteousness" or worth of Christ. Reconciliation is effected, estrangement healed. Through the God-Man man
becomes man once more; that is, he is restored to that
relationship which is at once the precondition and the
essence of his proper end. In the pregnant words of Ire-
naeus "Jesus Christ, on account of His great love, became
what we are that He might make us what He is Himself." [20] Since life is now accepted as a gift, man is free
to will the good without anxious self-regard. He is free
to make God's will his own in spontaneous gratitude for
the miracle of divine forgiveness. This is the real meaning of "sanctification." Whenever sanctification is understood as obligation, as a chore, it is being looked at from
the point of view of natural man, to whom God exists
in a juridical association. This concept is not, as such,
erroneous: natural man rightly apprehends that absolute
value has a total moral claim upon him. But it is a claim
which cannot be discharged as long as man deludes himself with the pretension that his striving will discharge it.
The dutiful will cannot "pull itself up by its own boot-
straps," for its attempt to do so is (as Luther in the mon-
astery found) invariably corrupted by the pride of merit.
It can only accept the power which comes to it from a
new relationship made possible by the justifying act of
God. Sanctification is not the cultivation of some "spiritual" quality immanent in man, neither is it the result of

a supernatural "medicine" infused into him, nor the mechanical response of God to Himself through the Holy Spirit. It is rather that regenerating potency which vitalizes those who know by faith that the favor they could never earn has, on God's prevenient initiative, been bestowed upon them as a free gift. This is not to denigrate the value of systematic, rationalized obedience or the disciplined practice of the Presence, for in this life not even the elect live on a perpctually sustained level of impulsive gratitude. But these things have no saving force. Their spring is the passion to glorify the One who has already declared the sinner righteous, his guilt "covered" by the expiating blood of the crucified God-Man.[21]

In saying that in the Atonement God imputes to man the worth of Christ, I mean not only that man is declared worthy but that he is also made worthy. That is, he is made capable of fulfilling in principle the end for which he was created. Not that he is rendered perfect, by any means, but that he finds in the Cross a dynamic which orients him towards perfection, motivating his free loyalty through the sheer attractive power of revealed grace.* With the restoration of communion, theosis becomes an authentic possibility because man can now love without selfish motivation. Noesis becomes a genuine potentiality because the regnant egoism which distorts man's vision is now removed. Personality becomes a realistic goal because self-centeredness, the only total barrier to self-realization, has now given way to God-centeredness. Participation in the Kingdom becomes an actuality because gratitude to God engenders love of neighbor.

The love of neighbor is the social fruit of the Atonement, motivationally considered. Inasmuch as God loves

---

*"*Thou didst desire man's free love, that he should follow Thee freely, enticed and taken captive by Thee.* In place of the rigid ancient law, man must hereafter with free heart decide for himself what is good and what is evil, having only Thy image before him as his guide" (Fyodor Dostoyevsky, *The Brothers Karamazov,* trans. Constance Garnett, New York: Random House, 1950, p. 302). (Italics mine.)

us sacrificially and without regard to merit, we are challenged and to some degree empowered to love our neighbor in the same way. Fletcher discerningly observes that "to love Christianly is a matter of attitude, not of feeling." [22] Christian love has nothing to do with liking; if it did, it would be an emotion, and therefore could not be commanded. It is rather the non-affective disposition to deal lovingly with the neighbor whether we like him or not. Such love, which manifests itself in service, is the inclusive social vocation to which every Christian is called. As Luther puts it,

> in all his works he should be guided by this thought and look to this one thing alone, that he may serve and benefit others in all that he does, having regard to nothing but the need and advantage of his neighbor.[23]

Yet it cannot be too strongly emphasized that this is not something which the neighbor is entitled to claim as a right. It is quite true that the divine example teaches the redeemed "to attribute worth without necessarily first finding it in those to whom they are duty-bound by Christ." [24] But this no more establishes a rightful claim upon our sacrificial love by the neighbor than the imputation of worth to us by God establishes a rightful claim upon His sacrificial love by us. The only right established in either case is the functional freedom correlative to the capacity for the fulfillment of a proper end. To those to whom God imputes worth, this right is imputed as a necessary inference. To those to whom the redeemed attribute worth, it is attributed as a necessary inference. But as for the self-giving love which issues in positive service, it is a pure gratuity which the redeemed dare not demand of God, nor the neighbor of the redeemed. "Agapē goes out to our neighbors not for our own sakes nor for theirs, really, but for God's." [25] Service of the neighbor is a duty owed *toward* not *to* the neighbor; he has no right to claim it, for it is owed to God alone. Failure to appreciate this vital point has probably been productive of more mischievous confusion than anything else in the whole history of Christian social ethics. It is, for example, the source of such vagaries as Reinhold Niebuhr's unmistakable implication that the criminal has a "right" to be forgiven.[26]

Although the above distinction has been largely overlooked, it received penetrating treatment at the hands of the Victorian philosopher James Martineau. Entombed in the second volume of his *Types of Ethical Theory,* a work long out of print, his masterful discussion of the topic at hand deserves wide currency. For this reason, despite its length, I feel justified in quoting it in full, and shall consider my book successful if it does nothing more than to rescue this eloquent and thoughtful passage from its unwarranted oblivion:

> It is sometimes said, by humane but inexact moralists, that since all obligation rests at bottom on the same foundation, charity is as much a claim upon us as justice, and that we violate a right not less when we neglect to fly to the relief of distress, than if we were to steal a neighbour's purse. The difference, it is contended, goes no deeper than this; that in the latter case it is found practicable to enforce the right by coercion of law; while in the former it is not; but the absence or presence of positive enactment is a mere affair of external machinery, leaving the inner essence of the two duties still the same. The truth and falsehood contained in this doctrine easily fall asunder at the touch of the principle just laid down [that in our relations to men, "the authoritative measure of duty, in every transaction between different persons, is the *mutually understood ideal"*]. *As between man and man,* it is not true that the claim to justice and to mercy are of equal validity, discriminated only by the possibility or impossibility of redress in case of default; no right being established without a common moral sense, or having any social measure except that of mutual understanding, there is a vast interval between the obligation which I have openly incurred in the face of my neighbour's conscience and that which is only privately revealed to my own. Over and above the intrinsic guilt in both instances, there is in the first the

additional enormity of violated good faith; and though, on the one hand, it is the sign of a mean and grudging nature to limit the measure of duty to the positive and authorised expectations of others from us, it would be, on the other, a monstrous paradox to say, that those expectations make no difference to us, and add no intensity to the claim upon us. Were it so, there would be no means of graduating offenses, or deciding between conflicting suggestions of right; and we should relapse into the Stoic fallacy of reducing to one level the most trivial omission and the greatest crime. . . .

In proportion then, and only in proportion, as men have come to understand concurrence on matters of right, have they claims *inter se.** This concurrence is far from being limited to relations of property and contract, although it is there most definite and complete: it extends over an indeterminate field beyond, of obligation prevailingly acknowledged, but differently construed, and unsusceptible, from its shifting complexity of conditions, of reduction to precise general enactment. The right of my neighbour, measured from the simply human and social point of view, addresses me with every variety of distinctness and force throughout this scale; with unmistakable emphasis in case of explicit engagement; with clearness perfectly adequate in cases of implicit trust; with evanescent faintness in cases of simply spontaneous whispers within my own conscience, with nothing corresponding in his presumed feeling and expectation. This very whisper, however, which involves no understanding with others, is itself an understanding *between myself and God,* and constitutes therefore an articulate obligation in relation to Him, not one whit

---

*We have no claims as such against transgressors with whom we share no "mutually understood ideal." This is why that person who is adjudged unable to distinguish between right and wrong cannot be held legally responsible for his acts. Yet his innocence does not make him the less subject to coercive restraint. Against such individuals, as against "breeds without the law" (i.e., communities outside of and hostile to the common ideal), the community of concurrence on matters of right is obliged to take defensive measures for its own survival, and in principle such measures may, in cases of extremity, justifiably extend even to the extermination of the innocent predator. Those who stand outside the law are not entitled to its protection, and when they threaten it, must be dealt with with whatever rigor its security requires. But such rigor cannot be a matter of retributive justice, only of defense.

less religiously binding on me than the most palpable debt of integrity. Its simple presence in the soul with its authoritative look is sufficient to establish it as a Divine claim upon me. In this aspect, it is quite true that all duty stands upon the same footing; and that all transgressions are offenses against the same law. But it is not every unfaithfulness to God that constitutes a violation of the rights of men, and gives them a title to reproach us. In forgetfulness of this distinction, the satirist frequently taunts religious persons with confessing before God sins which they would be very angry to have charged upon them by men; and evidently regards this as a proof of insincerity or self-deception. But surely there is here no real, scarcely even any apparent, inconsistency. The claims of God upon us, coextensive with our own ideal, go far beyond the claim of men, which is limited, we have seen, by the range of mutual moral understanding, and which in turn limits their critical prerogative of censorship and accusation. And Conscience, in seeking peace with Him, must needs have a very different tale to tell from any that transpires in settling the narrower accounts with them; and should they thrust themselves in to that higher audit, and demand to have its sorrowful compunctions addressed to them, it needs no spiritual pride to be hurt by the impertinence. Human society may punish us for *crimes;* human monitors reprove us for *vices;* but God alone can charge upon us the *sin,* which He alone is able to forgive. Far from believing that religious sincerity and depth would gain by the erasure of this distinction, I am convinced that its scrupulous preservation is a prime essential to their continuance at all, and needs to be enforced rather than enfeebled. There is a certain morbid and confused Christian humility which is not content with deploring, in the sight of Heaven, its failure in humane and charitable zeal, but speaks of it as a *wrong done* to others, as a witholding *of a debt due* to the unhappy and neglected and depraved, whose forgiveness is almost asked for the slight they have sustained. I would not deal ungently with any recognition of brotherhood among the separated classes of our modern civilization. But this language is not true, and tends to disturb the incidence of human responsibility, and fill with the notion of claims and rights those who much rather need to be awakened to their duties. To reform the thief and drunkard, to train the abandoned child, to succour the miseries of the improvident, is indeed a duty; not however *to them*, for their claim looks elsewhere, and we do but pick up a *dropped obligation*;—but to God and His moral order of the world. The total loss of this idea from the humanistic school of writers in the present day is the great draw-back on the purity of their influence. The defect springs from the preponderance of social geniality over ethical and spiritual conviction; but the infection has been caught by evangelical philanthropy; and the danger is not slight of establishing the worst element of socialistic feeling in the minds of men, viz. the demand that the duties of one class shall be performed for them by an-other, and that institutional machinery shall be created to supersede the patient toil and sacrifice of all house-holds and all persons, taken one by one. Let but the same ministrations of charity issue from an inspiration higher than compassion, and be rendered to the Divine order instead of to human confusion and wretchedness; and there will be a wholesomeness and dignity in our humanities, rarely traceable in them now. In this higher department of duty, scarcely less than in the minor cares that else would become flat and mean, it is impor-tant to the balanced and sustained force of the soul to render our service "not as unto men, but unto God." [27]

Charity is a debt we owe to God. He wills that it be paid to men instead. But men do not deserve it. For them to demand it as a right is presumption; for society to en-force it is usurpation. But for us to refuse to give it is undutiful and impious.

Having thus distinguished between gratuities and rights on the human level, we are faced with the problem of determining to whom rights apply. For if human rights are grounded upon Christ's Atonement, this question naturally arises: do only His elect possess rights? Or are all men possessed of rights through the Atonement? It does not lie within our sphere of discourse to speculate as to whether the soteriological efficacy of the Atonement is limited or universal.* For the sake of argument I propose here simply to assume that it is limited, since if it were universal the question of the non-elect would be precluded, and I wish to treat of every possibility. My answer is that whereas, strictly speaking, only the elect may be said to possess rights "de jure" (because only they have been rendered potentially capable of realizing the end for which they were created) , rights accrue "de facto" also to the non-elect. This is because there is no absolute, objective human means of determining who are elect and who are not. Hence, rights must be attributed to all who accept their correlative obligations, first among which is the willingness to abide by the regulating principle of reciprocity. Furthermore, God's will for the elect projects a general social order in which mutual rights for everyone are pragmatically presupposed. Rights are functional, and service is the function of the elect. Since only the elect can be purely motivated to glorify God, they alone may be regarded as having true personal callings and the functional rights which pertain thereto. But anyone who performs a necessary function in society has an impersonal calling which carries with it the right to the freedom requisite to its exercise.† And in order that the elect may have liberty to serve, all men must be accorded liberty as such.

For himself, who alone has any genuine personal claim to rights, he who is redeemed claims nothing, for he is committed to the example of the One whose worth has been imputed to him. But the fact that he is thus bound to renounce them for himself establishes his initial claim all the more firmly, since nothing can be renounced which is not first possessed. It is in terms of his priesthood that every Christian must insist upon his rights—his free-

---

*I concur with Emil Brunner's treatment of this subject. See his *Christian Doctrine of God,* trans. Olive Wyon (Philadelphia: Westminister), pp. 308–313.

†This right, too, is the fruit of grace, for it stems from God's undergirding concern for social order.

dom to worship God by *ministering* to the needs of others. Here, equally, he looks to the precedent of his divine Exemplar, who would not be constrained from healing on the sabbath. His meekness turns to adamant as he contends for the just prerogatives of his high calling. Whosoever seeks to thwart him here dare not anticipate the bowed head nor the averted cheek, lest he be stopped short by the majestic intransigence of Christian freedom with its stern rebuke: "Wist ye not that I must be about my Father's business?" [28]

*Part Two—The Community of Covenant*

## Chapter Five

# The Primal Right as the Bond of Covenant

Let us inquire further into what is meant by the assertion that God's will for His elect projects a social order in which rights for everyone are presupposed. To begin with, we must bear in mind the social dimension of the end of human existence, earlier identified as *sobornost* or community. Community is the matrix of free, cooperative relationships within which personality is shaped; conversely, it is the horizontal plane upon which personality finds expression. Its epitome and crown is communion with God, but this communion is anticipated by and reflected in loving association among human beings. Such is the Kingdom of God, the goal to which the recognition of human rights is instrumental.

I have defined a right as a functional relationship between value and obligation. Rights do not exist in a vacuum: they assume a context in which moral decisions are arrived at. Rights are therefore relative to context. But every context is a field in which not only do relative values compete with one another but also in which absolute value makes its claim. The right of absolute value is an absolute right as over and against all other rights. As Fletcher tells us, "there must be an absolute or norm of some kind if there is to be any true relativity." [1]

In Fletcher's "Christian situationalism" this norm is

"agapēic love," and he rightly holds that there is but one inflexible maxim by which rights are validated: the commandment to love one's neighbor—i.e., to will his welfare for God's sake, and deal with him accordingly wherever the concrete occasion may arise. But he also recognizes that the neighbor whose welfare one is thus obliged to maximize is Everyman, not merely the immediate neighbor, the one who simply happens to be nigh. Because the term "neighbor" in this sense embraces all humanity, love must be distributed with forethought, lest it be randomly bestowed on some at the expense of others. Thus Fletcher coins the aphorism: "Justice is love distributed; nothing else." [2] He believes that in order to find a regulative principle for its own distribution, love must form a coalition with utilitarianism to produce the "agapēic calculus"—the greatest amount of welfare for the largest possible number of neighbors.

The "humane but inexact moralists" deplored by Martineau, who blur the distinction between charity and justice, do both a palpable disservice. While in charity love goes beyond justice, justice is at the same time love's most imperative and unconditional demand. Love incorporates justice but justice does not incorporate charity. To define it as if it did, as, for instance, Ramsey does,[3] is to stultify love itself by misinterpreting the nature of what it calls for first and foremost. "Justice is love distributed" among competing claims, but rights provide the norm for distribution. Before love can be equitably bestowed upon those whose only claim is need, claims based upon rights must first be satisfied, and mere need does not establish rights.

Fletcher is to be commended for his insistence that where more than one neighbor is affected, the responsible exercise of love requires its rational distribution. His agapēic calculus, however, is open to the same serious objection which has been raised against Bentham's attempt to quantify felicity: that the greatest good of the greatest number does not necessarily square with the greatest quantity of good.[4] Bentham himself (if the relevant passages in his posthumous *Deontology* can be attributed to him rather than to his editor) finally came to realize that the felicity of a majority, if gained at too great expense to that of the minority, will reduce that of the whole.[5]

Furthermore, the fact that there are other neighbors than the immediate, particular neighbor, suggests that there are also wider contexts than the immediate, particular context. The human situation is itself a context—a universal context which calls for a universal framework for love's optimal expression. Where this framework is at issue, circumstances never alter cases. This is why justice is personified as wearing a blindfold. Kant deserves honor for his rigorous fidelity to this insight, even if his illustrations of it were not always tenable. Yet it was never more forcefully elucidated than by David Hume, who represents the antithesis of Kant's ethical formalism:

> however single acts of justice may be contrary either to public or private interests, it is certain that the whole plan or scheme is highly conductive, or indeed absolutely requisite, both to the support of society, and to the well-being of every individual. Though in one instance the public be a sufferer, this momentary ill is amply compensated by the steady prosecution of the rule, and by the peace and order which it establishes in society. And even every individual person must find himself a gainer on balancing the account; since, without justice, society must immediately dissolve. . . .[6]

This is what Fletcher does not understand. He tells us that "situation ethics keeps principles sternly in their place, in the role of advisers without veto power"; that "it deals with cases in all their contextual particularity, deferring in fear and trembling only to the rule of love"; that "love's decisions are made situationally, not prescriptively"; and that "when the impersonal universal conflicts with the personal particular, the latter prevails in situation ethics." [7] So fearful is he of wooden legalism that he does not see that his own emphasis upon the need for responsible distribution implies a need for a long-range, generalized perspective.

Love's most primary and categorical task, which takes precedence over the effectuation of any particularistic sum of welfare, is the building up and preservation of the universal framework for its own optimal exercise—a framework which is geared neither to the isolated good of a single neighbor nor to that of the greatest number but to the whole, neither to an immediate context nor to a more distant one but to the generic and eternal requirements of the human situation. The only way in which love can minister distributively to the concrete needs of persons is through a framework which, precisely because it is abstract and impersonal, insures that persons not be treated arbitrarily.

This does not mean, of course, that obligation can be reduced to a set of intrinsically binding rules, all equally absolute in their authority, for if more than one rule is absolute we are left without a guide in case of conflict. What it means is that every concrete occasion for the exercise of neighbor-love is set in a universal context, the demands of which are morally prior to all else. It means that there is implicit in the love commandment one rule which admits of no exception, regardless of the suffering its application may create in any given case: *the framework must be fostered at all costs.* What is this framework? It is what John F. A. Taylor speaks of as the "community of covenant" based on "the articles under which men are capable of standing in permanent and voluntary relations with one another." [8] It is the order within which rights are recognized and given force.

Were this order not profoundly impersonal, that is to say impartial and general, it would be hostile rather than encouraging to personality. Personality demands a government of laws and not of men. We mistakenly attribute depersonalization to the impersonality of abstract relationships, forgetting that their impersonality is an aspect of their rationality, and that the alternative to rationality is arbitrariness. Nothing is more depersonalizing than to be subject to persons rather than to laws. It is errant romantic nonsense to suppose, for example, that a feudal economic structure based on personal fealty and patronage is more conducive to personal dignity than is a structure of free contractual relationships based on the law of supply and demand. When people urge the "humanizing" of economic relationships, i.e., the imposition of extraneous personal considerations upon the operation of the market, what they are really advocating is paternalism, which demeans personality by substituting for the free exchange of goods and services an association between dependent and patron. This association, it may be parenthetically remarked, is not less demeaning when the patron, instead of being an individual, is a collective or official entity. Contrary to the popular delusion, there is no magic which can transmute a contemptible relationship to one of honor simply because the state is party to it. Paternalism is degrading to all but children, regardless of by whom it may be dispensed. William Graham Sumner somewhere exclaims in his characteristically astringent fashion that what is most needed is not to inject sentiment into our industrial relationships but to take it out of them.

Routinization and depersonalization are not the same. The division of labor, in the complex form which marks its mature development and upon which all the personality-liberating richness of advanced civilization rests, requires the performance of minutely specialized activity, much of which is doubtless boring. It is a superficial and atomistic notion of personality which would insist that personality demands that such activity give way to the more intrinsically satisfying production of individually crafted goods. Responsible personality is strengthened not impaired by willingness to shoulder the humdrum duties necessary to the accomplishment of worthwhile ends, and truly creative vision is not thwarted by the apparent insignificance of immediate tasks however monotonously repeated, but looks beyond them to the harmony of functions of which they are a part.

Only an impersonal framework can provide for the fullest growth of the human relationships which make for personality's burgeoning and fulfillment. The principles of public order most favorable to love's optimal exercise are necessarily general and abstract. They are the principles of justice, and justice is no respecter of persons. Yet justice enhances personal dignity and fosters genuine communion because instead of leaving the individual with nothing to rely upon but sentiment and subjective impulse, it creates a stable field of mutual expectation within which voluntary cooperation finds free play and ample scope, opening the way to deeper levels of creative fellowship.

• • •

All other rights arise from the right of value to external freedom in its self-expression. The social significance of the Atonement is that since God imputes value to those whom He has called, and since there is no sure human criterion for ascertaining their identity, value must be in practice attributed to all men. This means that all men must be accorded, mutually, the right to freedom.

No one measures up empirically to the norm for full humanity, and we cannot arrogate to ourselves the office of fixing boundaries to the graciousness of God. Therefore no empirical considerations can justify the presumption of classifying anyone as less than human. Even those who appear, because of rational deficiency, manifestly incapable of performing any distinctively human function, cannot directly for this reason be in principle denied the freedom correlative to such performance. However, liberty is complementary to responsibility. If minority, idiocy, or insanity renders a person unaccountable because he has not yet learned enough or is unable to learn from experience and guide his actions by the knowledge thus acquired, he must be subjected to such restraint as may be necessary to protect others from the burdens which, if allowed free reign, his lack of foresight and judgment would assuredly impose. This is merely an inference from the reciprocity of genuine freedom: he who is helpless to restrict his use of freedom so that it will not interfere with that of others, must have it restricted for him, and with anyone who cannot be held responsible for his actions this is presumptively the case. Furthermore, those who bring a child into the world have obligated themselves to prepare him for independence when he comes of age. This obligation can be fulfilled only through tutelage and the temporary limitations on his freedom which it necessarily entails.

It is, of course, impossible to fix with absolute precision the point at which an individual can be regarded as responsible and therefore fit for freedom. There are, however, objective criteria for determining, in a general and approximate way, whether or not people are possessed of sufficient experience and rationality to be able to know what consequences are reasonably assignable to actions, and to be amenable to normal prudential sanctions. This touchstone need not entail a very expansive view of the role which reason plays in human conduct; a fairly modest standard will suffice: the mere capacity to understand that certain actions will bring legal penalty, and impulses not so imperious as to be ungovernable by such understanding. Hayek rightly says that if freedom is to fulfill its aim, such minimum capacity must in the absence of clear disproof be attributed to all who satisfy certain objectively ascertainable tests (such as age), together with the status of being free and responsible members of the community.[9] As for those who do not satisfy such tests or whose capacity is disproved, there is no moral warrant for restricting their freedom beyond whatever degree may be individually required for their tutelage or safety or the security of others.

No one who enjoys the free status reserved for those presumed to be responsible can claim immunity from the accountability correlative to that status. That a person is presumed responsible implies that he is presumed susceptible to the deterrent impact of anticipated retribution. Retribution means two things: first, that the "community of covenant" is deadly serious about its mutually understood ideal, and will not tolerate the violation of that ideal by any of its members; second, that the dignity of accountability is not withheld from the transgressor. The commission of an aggressive anti-social act does not automatically or even ordinarily justify the assumption that its agent was incorrectly presumed to be responsible. Nothing is more fatal to a free society than to assume that members who violate its covenants necessarily demonstrate thereby mere imbecility or servitude to environmental pressures or aberrant impulses which lie outside the scope of their control. Such assumption not only weakens irreparably the fabric of stable social expectations, but also ignores the fact that predatory acts are commonly preceded by a calculation of probable consequences which is not less rational and prudential for being, in cases where the predator is caught, inaccurate.

In his famous essay, *On Liberty,* the younger Mill sets forth the principle that "the sole end for which mankind are warranted, individually or collectively, in interfering with the liberty of any of their number, is self-protection," which is another way of saying that the only legitimate reason for interfering with freedom is to protect freedom. He then qualifies the range of this principle by stating that it "is meant to apply to human beings only in the maturity of their faculties." [10] I have attempted to demonstrate that to restrict the freedom of those whose faculties are undeveloped or diseased does not, in fact, place them outside the application of the principle, but is rather a necessary aspect of its application, just as is the restraint and punishment of conscious and deliberate predators. Unless freedom is reciprocally distributed, it operates oppressively on those who do not share it to the same extent as others. Therefore no one can be entrusted with freedom who cannot or will not observe the rule of reciprocity. The demands of freedom itself make it essential to deny him freedom. The principle of non-interference does not cease to apply to him; instead it but affects him in a special way, necessitated by its regulative norm and the peculiar nature of his own condition.

. . .

If it be said that the self-expression of human value does not necessarily require personal freedom, that conditions of external oppression often bring out the best in men, one may reply that while this may conceivably be true in certain exceptional cases, it certainly is not true in general. For every Aesop or Epictetus who achieves mature nobility in bondage, a thousand others have been spiritually dwarfed beneath the lash. For every Polycarp or Latimer for whom martyrdom evokes his finest hour, a thousand Galileos have recanted publicly that they might continue to create privately. For every St. Paul or John Bunyan who produces inspired masterworks in prison, a thousand flames of genius have been stifled by confinement. As for the handful whom oppression does not daunt, who can say but that their contribution might not be still greater in a setting of liberty? The *Ethics* of Dietrich Bonhoeffer and the *Diary* of Anne Frank cannot be read as arguments in favor of the circumstances under which they were brought into existence. As Hocking remarks,

> the conditions of our ignorance . . . will not permit us to assume, will never permit us to assume, that human powers develop as well in servitude as in freedom: the presumption will always be on the other side.[11]

Even if it should be demonstrated that the growth of character thrives upon the rigors of persecution, this would no more justify slavery than martial heroism justifies war. Behind the barbed wire of the concentration camp the old man presses his priceless store of powdered milk upon the wan mother and her sickly child. Behind the bars of Reading Gaol the prisoner feels the murderer's fate as if it were his own. In the House of the Dead compassion lives. It lives in the tapping of a monocle against a cell wall; in the crumpled note, furtively secreted; in the muffled whisper, exhorting, "Courage!" Where love is present it will find a way to manifest itself. But surely it is not God's will that human brotherhood be limited to cramped, clandestine modes of demonstration. A tap on the wall, a whisper in the night—these may be earnests of the fullness of the Kingdom, but they are also prophetic judgments upon any social order which necessitates them.

• • •

Hocking tells us that an individual has an absolute right to become what he is capable of becoming.[12] I am forced to agree with LeBoutillier's verdict that "this right appears to be more relative than absolute. For a man to become the best that he potentially can become might and would entail unreasonable and devastating sacrifices on the part of others." [13] (In fairness to Hocking it should be said that in the actual development of his position, he provides safeguards against this contingency. However, they are not implicit in the principle itself.) Russell Kirk observes with reference to the United Nations Universal Declaration of Human Rights that "if a man has a *right* to marry, some woman must have the duty of marrying him; if a man has a *right* to rest, some other person must have the duty of supporting him." [14] The "right to marry" really means, of course, the freedom of persons so inclined to marry one another provided that their doing so does not place involuntary burdens upon third parties. Similarly, the "right to rest" means the freedom to do so as long as it does not inflict involuntary expense on someone else. Whatever their intention as to the former right, it seems obvious that the drafters of the Universal Declaration had in mind a vastly more ambitious connotation for the latter than the one which I have just set forth.

When properly qualified, the "right" to realize one's legitimate potentialities disappears as such. There remains only the right to mutual freedom in the pursuit of their realization. This freedom is the primal right from which all others spring. It is anterior to and a necessary prerequisite for the unhampered operation of voluntary cooperative relationships and the rationalized enjoyment and development of all other social goods. If it be violated even in the most minute particular for the sake of some other good, a precedent has been set for the negation of that upon which the stability of every social good rests. Thus no man can be said to have a right to the positive fulfillment of his end (even if that end be seen functionally in terms of selfless service to the neighbor), for such would inevitably trench upon the freedom of others to seek the fulfillment of their ends, undermining the structure of mutual non-interference which provides the only rational criterion for adjudicating competing claims to personal fulfillment.

Christian ethicists of the dominant outlook are fond of describing the philosophy of limited government as "nihilistic." But the real nihilist is the one who would substitute for the precious structure of mutual non-interference, some form of unrestricted political sovereignty tempered, one would hope, by the benevolence of those who wield it. Doctrinaire socialism seems to have lost its vogue among the more sophisticated leaders of ecumenical Protestantism; even Reinhold Niebuhr now declines to defend his early dependence upon Marxist dogma.[15] Yet they offer nothing in its place but a patchwork of ad hoc improvisations, derived from vague "middle axioms" which are often pragmatically incompatible and which lack any standard for hierarchical arrangement. Their disillusionment with full-fledged socialism has not brought them to the realization that reciprocal freedom is the only stable basis for community; instead, they put forth their bewildering welter of temporary and relative solutions under the banner of "A Responsible Society." [16]

LeBoutillier has already given us the clue as to why it is precisely that the positive fulfillment of man's end is not admissible as a right to be enforced: it does not provide for any regulating principle in cases of conflict. Let it not be supposed that even a triumphant reign of agapē would totally eliminate such conflict and obviate the need for such a principle. Whoever has observed the mutual rivalry of worthy benevolences knows that the purest motives are no proof against the inexorable fact that whereas the number of deserving aspirations is infinite, the resources with which to satisfy them are distinctly limited. Even the saints must have recourse to the standard of reciprocal freedom in defining the boundaries of their respective areas of charity and service.

What an individual needs apart from freedom in order to fulfill his proper end, cannot be objectively determined by any reliable criterion. We must depend either upon his own subjective assessment or upon the arbitrary decision of some authority. There would be no limit to the positive advantages an individual might demand for himself, nor would there be any bounds to the potential absolutism of any political agency entrusted with the power of such decision. Only freedom, as reciprocal, is capable of rational apportionment and exact juristic delineation.

When I speak of freedom I refer to freedom of the person and its various extensions from positive coercion. I emphatically do not refer to such nebulous and subjective concepts as "freedom from want" and "freedom from fear." To make the implementation of these a responsibility of government is to give precedence to so-called "rights" which are not reciprocally based and which have no dependable standard over a fundamental universal right susceptible of measurement.* Moreover, since it is axiomatic that man's wants are unlimited, any government which seriously undertook to guarantee "freedom from want" would need unlimited power. Even if its power were unrestrained by constitutional or other political limitations, it still could not succeed, for the limitations imposed by Nature would remain. As for "freedom from fear," it is hard to see how a government could assure it short of enforcing mass lobotomization.

Kant understood that man is inwardly free only as he submits to moral law. The self-mastery whereby the will fulfills itself through obedience to the command of duty he denominated "positive freedom." But he apprehended that politics is fitly concerned only with "negative freedom"—reciprocal freedom from external constraint.[17] In this he displayed a perspicuity superior alike to that of his direct philosophical successors and to that of his progenitor, Rousseau. The burden of Isaiah Berlin's great inaugural address at Oxford, as also of Talmon's monumental studies, is very largely to remind us that the attempt to make "positive freedom" the immediate responsibility of the state is fraught with consequences which reduce all freedom to a nullity.[18]

I have emphasized that rights are functional, and that freedom cannot therefore be regarded as an end in itself insofar as the vocation of the individual is concerned. This is not to say, however, that the political body has any higher purpose than to secure the "negative freedom" of its citizens. Personal fulfillment requires that freedom be directed toward an object that transcends the self, ul-

---

*"If you define a world with two wills in it, and with an insufficient supply of goods and consequent unsatisfied wants, it is not obvious that either will ought to give way to the other, or that each should do so. So long as they are two wills, related in such wise that the altruism of one is the egoism of the other, the idea of obligation cannot be extracted from the situation. I cannot find it in the simple fact of my neighbor's existence and his want" (W. E. Hocking, *Human Nature and Its Remaking*, rev. ed.; New Haven: Yale University Press, 1923, Appendix II, p. 481).

timately to that Object, which, as Supreme Subject, transcends all selves. But it does not fall within the province of the state to choose this object for the self. This is why there is a danger in the establishment of a "Commission on National Goals," as was done under the Eisenhower administration. The only legitimate goal of any nation as a political unit is that of insuring the reciprocal freedom of its citizens to pursue goals of their own choosing.[19]

Fabians such as Tawney[20] and Laski[21] place great stress upon the functional character of rights. Their error does not lie in this; it lies in their assumption that political authorities can manipulate justly the distribution of rights according to arbitrary ideas about the relative social desirability of various functions. The best intentions cannot render such manipulation just. Not only does it make a mockery of freedom but it leads to economic chaos. No one has yet devised a means superior to the free market of determining the relative social desirability of functions. As von Mises has irrefutably argued, only a free market makes rational economic calculation possible.[22]

L. T. Hobhouse demonstrates in a closely reasoned passage that although self-determination may be something more than the mere absence of external constraint, it can never be anything less.[23] Any coercive effort to guarantee its positive aspects undermines the negative foundation which is its unqualified precondition. This is why "beyond maintaining justice, the state [cannot] do anything else without transgressing justice." [24]

The worth of human beings is not predicated upon their acts; it is, however, exhibited in them. God's elect are distinguished by an ardor to show forth His glory in selfless deeds of service. But an act performed under compulsion has no moral value for the agent. "The law may compel men to be just, but it cannot compel them to be brothers. Pity, mercy, love—these are works of grace in freedom, and not works of a compelling law." [25] Justice is love's first demand, and as such it is objectively good even when coercively enforced. But only that which stems from free volition can be *morally* good—i.e., good in terms of motivation. And when the expanding state, forgetful of its proper task of guaranteeing rights, engulfs whole spheres of service it is extending the borders of the Realm of Caesar at the expense of the territory of the Realm of Spirit.

# Particularizations of the Primal Right

Now that we have deduced the primal right from the theological premises apart from which it has no ultimate foundation, our arguments will, for the most part, cease to be directly theological. For in spelling out the implications of reciprocal freedom for particular areas of human conduct, we need be guided only by the evidence of social data and the rules of logical consistency. Our definitive social norm has been established by reference to divine authority. But to seek to ground proximate norms immediately upon religious insights rather than upon the rational considerations involved in the functional particularization of reciprocal freedom, would be to circumvent an order of priority which reflects, as I have tried to show, God's will. Similarly, although the function of a church building is ordained by a religious sanction, it would be a poor ecclesiastical architect who, instead of rationally articulating this function, based his design upon the dimensions of Solomon's temple or upon modules of the sacred number seven under the misapprehension that an overall religious function dictates some overtly religious criterion for each detail. Because of analogous misapprehensions many attempts to deal with social issues from a Christian standpoint have turned out to be futile, where not actually pernicious, exercises in piosity.

. . .

Anti-social behavior is not limited to the predatory violation of human rights. It may also be expressed in acts of malice which deprive persons of goods to which they have no actual right but which common decency would let them keep. It may be expressed in sins of omission, in callousness, in apathy, in reluctance to forgive. It may also be expressed in personal conduct which offends moral or aesthetic sensibilities but which does not infringe upon the freedom of others. These expressions do not fall within the purview of coercive action.

The legitimate competence of the state does not extend to the enforcement of benevolence, the regulation of private morals, or the compulsion of economic exchanges to which all parties do not enter voluntarily. For reasons which will become apparent later, this delimitation should not be understood to exclude certain types of intervention on behalf of the general public health and safety, the protection of minors and others not legally responsible for their own welfare, and the defensive requirements of the community. Nor should it be taken to imply that government cannot justly provide any positive services of a non-protective character. If such services are not operated as monopolies, and if their costs are borne exclusively by those who choose to use them, no coercion is involved. When government functions in this wise, it is merely acting as a voluntary cooperative association. While its expedience may be open to question, such a role is not morally objectionable. Neither, however, is it truly governmental in the sense in which the term has any significance within the context of this essay.

When quickened by the importunities of urgent and

pathetic need, the Christian conscience is tempted to turn to any remedy which promises fast relief. Especially is this true when the support of relief can be so distributed as to be scarcely felt by those who bear it, while in comparison the distress which calls for help is well-nigh crushing to its sufferers. But does this justify coercion? No need, however immediately vital, is more socially important from a long-range standpoint than is the need for a structure which guarantees respect for rights. I am willing, for the sake of argument, to concede that a hypothetically perfect structure of reciprocal freedom might not reduce involuntary poverty and its attendant ills to such restricted compass as to render their adequate alleviation within the practical capability of private eleemosynary effort. Yet the alleviation of misery is not, as such, a right, and ought not, as such, to be coercively enforced. For the use of coercion, other than to guarantee rights, is an infringement upon rights, and respect for rights is an absolute and over-riding desideratum.

The thoughtful person may sympathize with one who robs because of hunger, but he will not countenance robbery as a policy for the relief of want, since he realizes that such a policy would undermine the very possibility of mutual security and trust. An individual who embezzles money for the sake of charity is quite properly sent to jail if his defalcation is discovered, regardless of the humanity of his intent. Yet for many minds it would seem as if a benevolent object is all that is required to put the stamp of legitimacy upon robbery as long as it is perpetrated through the taxing power of the state. This double standard will not stand the test of moral scrutiny: stealing does not cease to be stealing when it is authorized for philanthropic purposes by vote. There is, in fact, a special culpability involved when the political agency is perverted to the execution of the very acts which it has been constituted to prevent.

The plight of the unemployed Appalachian coal miner

may be pitiable, but (unless it is union violence which prevents his working) he is not the victim of predatory interference with his freedom. It is the California taxpayer forced to subsidize the regional development of Appalachia who is the victim of such interference. Where slum conditions stem (as they so often do) from exploitive privilege sanctioned and abetted by law, this underlying causal factor should be rooted out by law. But injustice is compounded when the average suburbanite, wholly innocent of exploitation, is saddled with the burden of rehabilitating blighted neighborhoods and lives. It is no doubt sad when rural families are uprooted on account of massive changes in the nature of agricultural production. Yet this scarcely makes it fair that a levy should be placed on city dwellers in order to preserve artificially an economic unit which has lost its viability. The foundling, the abandoned mother, the aged pauper, the handicapped, those left destitute by earthquake, draught and fire, deprived by ignorance, or caught in the toils of technological unemployment—yes, even the victims of their own intemperance and folly—ought not be begrudged the sympathetic help of their compatriots. But the sword cannot exact relief for their distress without cutting into the essential underpinnings of a just society.

To assert that welfare services lie outside the proper competence of government is not to concede that they need be neglected or relegated to private individual performance. Why should it be taken for granted that things which individuals are unable, as individuals, to do for themselves must, if they are to be done at all, necessarily be done through the coercive power of government? Galbraith's dichotomy of national life into "public" (government) and "private" (individual and commercial) sectors presents a false, truncated picture of the possibilities.[1] Richard C. Cornuelle has latterly emerged as rediscoverer and prophet of a third category which he calls the "independent sector"[2]—that multitude of extralegal associations for voluntary cooperation in the pursuit of objects other than commercial profit, which de Tocqueville in the 1830s remarked as the most distinctive aspect of American society.[3]

With the increased complexity of social needs has come increasingly the abdication to government of the responsibility for their alleviation. It is taken as axiomatic that coercive, centralized authority is best equipped to deal with large and complex social problems. Yet the record is scarcely favorable to this assumption; indeed, it would seem rather to substantiate Walter Lippmann's early insight that the reverse is true: that coercive direction of human affairs becomes less effective in proportion as they become more intricate.[4]

From the Rochdale Society of Equitable Pioneers to Saul Alinsky's triumph of neighborhood rehabilitation "Back of the Yards," the voluntary group approach has demonstrated that it is not lacking in the potential to cope successfully with problems of human welfare. Even if this were not so, it would not necessarily follow that such problems should be handled by the state. To read a chronicle such as Gustavus Myers' *History of the Great American Fortunes* is to be impressed by the extent to which the maldistribution of wealth which lies behind so many social ills is traceable not to the natural processes of a free market but either to discriminatory or otherwise unjustified political intervention or to the dereliction by government of its true responsibilities.[5] If public authority, instead of lending coercive sanction to privilege, were to concentrate on its authentic duty of preventing it, the need for welfare services would, I have no doubt, be drastically reduced.

I think it doubtful that the incidence of vice would much increase if the state were to eschew the regulation of private morals. Vice has a way of evading regulation. It would, however, unquestionably become more overt and consequently in some ways more offensive. Yet the fact that something is offensive to most people does not make it properly subject to forcible suppression. I dare say that when someone in our presence picks his teeth, scratches himself obtrusively, or uses the back of his sleeve for a handkerchief, most of us experience reactions of distaste. But however much such conduct may outrage our sensibilities, it would never occur to us to advocate, even theoretically, its legal interdiction, for it does not constitute a violation of our rights. Why then should legal interdiction be applied to *any* type of grossness which offends not against rights but only against sensibilities? Drunkenness and gluttony, sexual lewdness, promiscuity and perversion may be grounds for social ostracism. They are not, in and of themselves, grounds for coercive interference. There are, of course, transgressions against taste and public decency which are at the same time transgressions against public safety, health and order, and which come properly therefore within the purview of the law. To pollute the atmosphere with noxious fumes is more than just a breach of etiquette. To disturb a neighborhood with raucous noise is more than just a breach of personal propriety. To transmit a venereal disease is more than just a breach of moral rectitude. Such actions are not merely unseemly or unconventional: they are unjust, and rightly subject to legal prohibition. It is also within the province of the state to protect the marriage covenant (as to protect contracts in general) and to restrict such sexual arrangements as may infringe upon the rights of offspring, actual or potential. This is why, for instance, incest (at least when procreation is a possibility) is justly forbidden by law. But apart from such considerations, there is no reason why the state should concern itself with whether or not people decide to formalize their sexual ties by marriage, whether or not they opt to confine their choice of erotic partners to members of the opposite sex, or whether or not they choose monogamy in preference to a harem.

Although I happen to live at present in the South, I am not personally a segregationist, and I believe that to refuse service, lodging or employment to a fellow human being on racial grounds is to be guided by criteria which normally should be irrelevant.* Yet I cannot see that such refusal represents a violation of any right, for it constitutes no predatory interference but only a decision to refrain from a certain type of contract or exchange. For the police power, on the other hand, to compel such contracts and exchanges is patently a violation of a right. No one disputes the prerogative of a customer or worker to discriminate among business establishments or employers, no matter how absurd may be the basis of discrimination. Should not, by the same token, a proprietor be similarly free to select his clientele, or an employer his workers? Of course, if an enterprise purports to serve the general public, it cannot rightfully deny service to anyone whose behavior is not aggressively disruptive, for to do so would be to fail to live up to its advertised policy, and would thus be, in effect, a breach of contract. But if it elects to serve only a restricted clientele, and publishes the fact, it cannot be accused of anything worse than churlish lack of catholicity—scarcely an offense which should be legally indictable.

The Montgomery bus boycott was an early landmark in the battle against racial inequality; its success first focused national attention upon Martin Luther King. It did not have recourse to the force of law but consisted simply in the concerted withdrawal of patronage from the city transit system by customers dissatisfied with the existing service. It was, in short, an exercise of the right to refrain from an exchange. But evidently King did not regard that right as other than a one-way proposition. In some measure because of his efforts and those of his associates, the principle of forced exchange has now been written into federal law. Were this principle generalized

---

*I say "normally" because in certain types of specialty enterprise, racial or ethnic factors may have a legitimate bearing upon optimum suitability for employment. A Chinese restaurant would be a case in point.

and impartially applied, the Montgomery bus boycott would today be legally impossible.

· · ·

Non-predatory expressions of social evil must be risked for the sake of the freedom without which moral goodness has no adequate outlet. However, the expression of evil which we call predation trespasses against that freedom itself, and thus threatens the very context for the good will's unimpeded exercise. This is why it can never be tolerated, and why it constitutes a fit subject for the restraining action of the law. The predator is answerable before the bar of human justice, not because his victim was necessarily in himself entitled to be left alone, but because predation undermines the pragmatic framework for a moral order. He is answerable before the bar of divine justice, not intrinsically because in harming an individual he has invaded man's rights, but because in interfering with that order he has invaded God's rights. For the rights of man have no reality apart from grace.

There are more facets to predation than may at first be obvious. Contract, property, and reputation are extensions of the person, and infringements upon these, no less than simple instances of bodily assault, are therefore violations of personal freedom. Let us now examine briefly the specific rights which are components of the primal right of freedom from predation, and the enforcement of which is the only legitimate office of the state as a coercive power. It is scarcely necessary to dwell upon the point that these, like the more general right from which they stem, are in principle self-limiting according to the contextual demands of reciprocity.

Rights do not admit of hierarchical arrangement, since at bottom they are one. Neither, for the same reason, can they conflict with one another. Only freedoms which are reciprocal can be considered rights, and no freedom is reciprocal which requires for its realization the violation of other freedoms. Where there is a conflict between apparent particularizations of reciprocal freedom, closer analysis will reveal that one or more of the competing particularizations is non-reciprocal and therefore false. For example, when freedom of expression is opposed to freedom from intrusion, the conflict is not actually a conflict between rights. Intrusive expression is not a particularization of reciprocal freedom, and is therefore not a right at all.

*1. The Right to Physical Integrity*    By "physical integrity," I mean freedom of the person proper from encroachment. Encroachment need not be malicious or even intentional to constitute a violation of this right. Thus manslaughter is justly classed a crime, and among the wrongs subsumed beneath the legal category of tort are some which partake of neither characteristic yet are quite meetly actionable. Nor need a violation involve direct physical contact; this right is transgressed as clearly by a "Typhoid Mary" as by a "Boston Strangler." Inasmuch as the communication of disease falls squarely within the margin of predation, the power to counteract predation is not misused if employed in the execution of such measures as quarantine, inoculation, and the enforcement of sanitary codes.

The production of stenches or disturbing noises also affronts the right to physical integrity, since they assault the sensory apparatus. The British understand far better than do we Americans that the right to freedom from intrusion is more fundamental than is the right to freedom of expression. They understand that the presumption of rectitude is against the one who acts; that all things being equal, he who is acted upon may justly claim priority of right. Although they accord unorthodoxy and eccentricity a high degree of tolerance, they do not countenance displays of self-expression which invade the privacy of others or disturb the peace.

While it is evident that individuals differ greatly in the extent to which their organs are offended, and that what is to one an irritation may be received with pleasure by another, this does not imply that the lowest common denominator ought always to be the criterion for prohibition. Even if all one's other neighbors sincerely enjoy listening to "rock-and-roll," the invalid across the street has an overriding right to quiet. And if the man across the street is not an invalid but merely deficient (or civilized!) in musical appreciation, his right should nonetheless take precedence. Obviously, however, such rights do not hold in all locations. He who frequents a discothèque cannot claim therein the right to quiet. He who visits a stockyard cannot claim therein consideration for olfactory fastidiousness. But unless an area is clearly zoned for such establishments, one may rightly demand that neither discothèque nor stockyard bring their peculiar emanations to one's vicinity.

There is, I concede, a point at which intrusion upon the person of another merges into mere offense to personal taste, ceasing to be a violation of the right to physical integrity. Perhaps this point can never be delineated with exactitude. The senses are indeed assailed by uncouth habits, yet I have already suggested that uncouth habits are not, in and of themselves, legitimately subject to forcible proscription. What of slovenly or vulgar dress? What of architectural monstrosities? What of advertisements which make one painfully aware of "denture breath," "uneasy bladder," and "B.O."? These are vexing questions, and I do not pretend to have discovered any absolute formula for resolving them. I have said that, all things being equal, he who is acted upon may justly claim priority of right. Yet I realize that allergies, phobias, and eccentric crotchets ought not be permitted to take precedence over general needs and feelings in a public context. In proportion as the context ceases to be private, there is probably no practical alternative but to accept the broadest sensory consensus as the norm for arbitration.

Before turning to the next category, I should be remiss were I to fail to mention a violation of physical integrity which, although until recently unknown, seems likely to become increasingly common unless prompt measures are taken to curtail it. I refer to that technique of mass persuasion which alters attitudes not by appeal to free volition but by subliminal conditioning. Since the subject is not consciously aware of what is being done to him, he is denied the opportunity to give or to withhold consent. One can scarcely imagine a more total and insidious invasion of the right of privacy.[6]

*2. The Right to Freedom of Expression* Just as the right to physical integrity forbids encroachment upon persons in states of relative passivity, the right to freedom of expression forbids encroachment upon non-predatory action, whether action in the form of movement or of speech and publication. I have already indicated that when the two conflict, the presumption of rectitude is against the actor. But this must be understood as relative to context, for there are times when passivity can constitute a violation of the right to peaceful movement. No one may legitimately claim the right to lie deliberately inert upon the sidewalk, to stand motionless so as to obstruct a doorway, or even to drive so slowly as to impede traffic.

Freedom to assemble is an important right, but there is no right to assemble in disregard of the laws of trespass, in defiance of the public peace, or in obstruction of the normal function of a given site. Public hallways are not maintained to accommodate "sit-ins," nor highways, to accommodate protest marches to the detriment of other uses.[7]

Freedom to associate is also an important right, but there is no right to impose oneself on people against their will. I grant that there are situations in which to deny superficial association to others would be to exclude them from access to goods which are of public right. But the mere proximity of another in a public place does not compel association in any sense repugnant to mutual freedom.

It is difficult for me to understand how anyone who champions the right of free association can contend that to associate for business purposes on a basis of limited liability is not a right but a privilege granted by the state. I am not prepared to take issue with Taylor's judgment as to the social dangers implicit in the divorce of control from responsibility, which he sees as characteristic of the modern corporation.[8] Nor have I any desire to deny the sharp distinction Walter Lippmann makes between the business corporation and natural and spontaneous associations bound together by kinship or fellowship.[9] But I do insist with Maitland that the state does not make a corporation by granting a charter any more than it makes a marriage by issuing a license.[10] In both cases all it does is to take legal cognizance of associations into which individuals enter not by the leave of an external power but by the mutual exercise of their own right of choice. It does not lie within the just province of the protective authority to say that individuals may or may not come together in a business relationship which proportions risk to ownership and vests control in employed managers. This is their prerogative, just as it is the prerogative of others to deal or to refrain from dealing with an establishment organized along such lines. And the protective authority is not justified in interfering any further in its operations that may be needful to prevent fraud or violence.

Freedom of movement implies liberty of travel and migration, but considerations of national defense may justify their restriction when the safety of the covenant requires it. A nation is not amiss in barring potential spies and saboteurs, or even in placing limitations on the movement of its own citizens in the interests of military security. It is furthermore by no means patent that the shelter of the covenant need be extended to unassimilable masses whose entry might go far to undermine it. I do not say this in a xenophobic spirit, for I am well aware that many foreign-born Americans are second to none in their devotion to the concept of reciprocal freedom which lies behind our fundamental institutions. My own grand-father was such a one. And I do not hesitate to term contemptible the policy of restricting immigration merely to perpetuate monopolistic wage levels through the shutting out of labor competition. An artificially-inflated living standard has no just claim against the rights of frugal and industrious folk who give no cause for disapproval other than their willingness to work for modest compensation. The fact remains, however, that an ethos which cherishes the covenant is the product of slow and painful evolution. Its vitality is precarious, for it is always threatened by that wanton and resentful multitude to whom membership in the covenant community is presumptively extended because of birth, but who are inwardly its foes. Dare we risk the peril which would surely come if to these native barbarians were precipitately added swarming millions fresh from lands in which the covenant has never found root, ignorant of our language and unschooled in the traditions of responsible self-government?

The right to unimpeded locomotion must likewise be qualified by consideration for the rights of property and tenure, shortly to be discussed. But all these qualifications, it should be borne in mind, are morally void except as necessary to the maintenance of mutual freedom. They are authoritative only as they issue either from respect for other particularizations of this primal right, or from solicitude for the framework within which rights are implemented. Thus arbitrary bondage to a fixed location (as in villeinage) has no moral warrant: it cannot be rationally deduced from the demands of mutual freedom. Neither can occupational restrictions based upon hereditary status.

What has been said about the movement of persons applies also to the movement of goods. Restrictions upon trade across national boundaries can be justified only by grave considerations of national defense. Apart from such considerations, tariffs and quotas constitute nothing more than a use of the police power to enforce favoritism—to give certain industries an artificial advantage at the expense of others and of the consumer. Governmental authority properly exists to provide protection against coercion, not against competition. It is ironic that so many protectionists are among the loudest panegyrists of competitive free enterprise, evidently seeing nothing inconsistent in their demand to be protected against the very thing they laud.\* This kind of protection violates not only the right to freedom of movement but also the right to ownership, for the right to ownership is sadly truncated unless it includes the right to unimpeded exchange.

The right to follow an occupation of one's own choosing may, as an inference from the right to free expression, seem too self-evident to call for mention. It *is* self-evident, perhaps, but not secure. Since for Marxism rights are only bourgeois fictions, we need not dwell upon the compulsory allotment of functions which obtains, at least in part, behind the Iron Curtain. In any case we scarcely have to range so far afield for our examples when occupational freedom here at home is thwarted by all manner of union, professional, and other monopolies encouraged and upheld by law. It is within the proper province of the police power to prohibit the deception of the public by means of false credentials and unfounded assertions as to occupational attainment. It is also doubtless necessary to enforce coercively such occupational standards as may be *genuinely* essential in the interests of general (as distinguished from private) health and safety. Certification may be justified as a device to prevent deception; licen-

---

\*An amusing instance is provided by a recent convention of the American Cattlemen's Association, as reported by the Associated Press. *(Birmingham News,* January 29, 1970.) Before going home, the 1,500 conventioneers expressed their concern "over the gradual deterioration of self-reliance we see in America," citing the cattleman as "one of a dwindling breed—the individualistic businessman who makes his living from the land," receiving no artificial props "including government subsidies." They also passed a resolution "demanding the federal government stand firm against reducing limits on importing meat so the American cattle industry can be preserved and the nation's consumer provided with high quality beef."

sure is justified only where incompetence produces dele-
terious neighborhood effects. It is questionable to me
whether the argument from neighborhood effects is so
definitive as to provide a reason why, except in very special circumstances, the practice of medicine or law, the
selling of real estate, the cutting of hair or the operation
of restaurants should be confined to persons licensed by
the state.[11]

Let it be emphasized, however, that freedom to pursue
an occupation of one's choice does not encompass any
title to assurance that one gain a livelihood by such pursuit. It does not encompass any title to assurance that occupational risks be mitigated by compulsory levy upon
others. It does not encompass any title to assurance that
ineptitude be subsidized, or skills for which there is no
market. Nor does it encompass any title to assurance that
opportunities for vocational preparation be made available at general expense.

And it must, of course, be qualified by the proviso that
one pursue one's occupation in such a way as to avoid trespass against one's neighbors. Thus occupations to which
trespass is intrinsic are obviously proscribed. No amount
of proficiency or temperamental aptitude could give a
man the right to be a buccaneer, a counterfeiter, or a
hired assassin. Neither has any one the right to use the
methods of such illegitimate careers in carrying on an
occupation in itself innocuous. No insect exterminator
has a right to "find" termites where none exist; no con-
tractor a right to grease palms so that inferior materials
will pass inspection; no retailer a right to misquote list
prices so as to give his selling prices the appearance of reduction; no workman a right to intimidate by threat of
violence his more industrious fellow into slackening his
pace.

The "right to work" is a slogan which had best be laid
to rest. Louis Blanc used it to popularize his ill-starred
scheme to do away with unemployment by providing
artificial jobs through government subvention. Today

we find it adopted by proponents of legislation which would outlaw the "closed shop." Occupational freedom, of course, implies the right not to be prevented coercively from working unless the public health or safety is thereby endangered. In this sense it is permissible to speak of the right to work, but rational discourse can profit little from the use of a phrase which lends itself to such diverse interpretation.

Occupational freedom implies also the right *not* to work, although this no more properly signifies the right to be supported while not working than the right to work properly signifies the right to have work artificially provided. Justice has nothing to say, however, against the voluntary withdrawal of labor from the market, regardless of whether that withdrawal be individual or collective, spontaneous or organized, so long as it does not occur in violation of contractual agreement and is not accompanied by coercion or intimidation. Although the laborer is not a commodity, his labor is *the* commodity par excellence, notwithstanding the wording of the Clayton Act (Section 6). Were this not so, he would be reduced to the indignity of mendicancy, for he would have nothing whatsoever to exchange.[12] Should he choose to withhold or withdraw it from the market, he has the same right to do so as has the owner of any commodity. In short, the right to strike is an aspect of the right to private property as well as of the right to occupational freedom. But the right to private property, it must be noted, belongs to the capitalist as well as to the worker. This raises grave questions as to the equity of restrictions pertaining to business monopoly resulting solely from size or mutual agreement (as distinguished from that which is created and/or given special protection by government), not to mention legislation prohibiting the lockout, the blacklist, and the "yellow dog contract." The argument for the right to strike is also an argument for the right of management to use its corresponding weapons of industrial conflict. As long as capital is forbidden to combine in restraint of trade, impartiality requires that similar combination on the part of labor be forbidden too. That business monopoly based solely upon combination be subjected to legal strictures from which labor monopoly so based is expressly exempted manifestly contradicts the principle of equality before the law. Should the proposal to remove such strictures raise the spectre of monopoly domination, it seems not inappropriate to cite the judgment of Walter Lippmann that "few effective monopolies have ever been organized and . . . none can long endure except where there is a legal privilege." [13]

Freedom of speech (which may here be broadly understood as to include all modes of communication) is no exception to the rule that any freedom ceases to be a right when exercised in such a manner as to invade the liberties of others or to threaten the covenental framework for the encouragement of mutual freedom. Even Justice Black, who esteems free speech so highly that he would attach no legal penalty to defamation, recognizes that the purchase of a ticket to the theater does not "buy the right to make a speech there." [14] Speech which of itself disrupts legitimate pursuits cannot be held inviolable; neither can speech which advocates predation. But if speech merely suggests ideas or excites passions without actually prescribing any predatory course of action, the onus is on its listeners alone should their reaction take a predatory form. Ivan Karamazov's cynical philosophizing planted a seed in the mind of Smerdyakov which led to murder. Yet in spite of Ivan's inward culpability, his crime was hardly one appropriate to come within the punitive cognizance of law. If an audience, provoked to anger by unpopular words, threatens the speaker with violence, its hostility is no just reason to arrest the speaker—as actually occurred in the Terminiello and Feiner cases. As long as they are not obliged to hear him, and presuming that he has not usurped the floor, a speaker's freedom ought not be diminished in proportion to his auditors' intolerance of what he says, regardless of the wrongness of his views. I cannot accept René Williamson's contention that the advocate of a "just" cause should be protected in his right to speak even if his speaking leads to riot, whereas the advocate of an "evil" cause has no such right.[15] It will be a sad day for freedom when protection is dependent upon subjective valuations of this sort. But perhaps I misconstrue Williamson: his illustration of an "evil" speech depicts malicious falsehood, which is, of course, a species of predation.

As Mill is careful to point out at the outset of his essay *On Liberty*, it is one thing to argue for free speech on grounds of social utility, and quite another to defend it as a right. Willmoore Kendall is correct in saying that much confusion would be avoided were current writers on the topic as scrupulous as Mill in the observance of this distinction.[16] Kendall perceptively observes that when free speech is thought of as a right, it is

> inconceivable save as one component of a system or complex of rights, that mutually limit and determine one another and are meaningless save as they are deemed subject to the general proposition that we are not entitled to the discharge of *any* right unless we discharge the duties correlative to that right.[17]

That is to say, it is only within the covenant that freedom of speech or any other freedom can be demanded as a right; if free expression is accorded either to those who would avowedly destroy the covenant by force, or to those who merely decline to bear their share of its support, it can only be as a matter of expedience and not of right. No one who advocates the violent overthrow of a libertarian constitution has a *right* to claim its immunities even in the harmless conduct of his ordinary affairs, much less in the expression of that advocacy. But there are persuasive reasons for insisting that only "clear and present danger" of the utmost gravity can make it expedient to deny him such immunities. While a free market in ideas does not by any means insure that truth and wisdom will prevail, the absence of a free market goes far to insure that they will not. Restraints upon the orderly expression of opinion are therefore, in the absence of overriding situational considerations to the contrary, socially disadvantageous even when such expression has no title to be regarded as a right.

*3. The Right to the Observance of Contracts*  I have already alluded to freedom of association as an aspect of freedom of expression. Since contract is a mode of association, freedom of contract need not be presented as a separate topic. The fact, however, that the right of contract would be meaningless without the concomitant obligation to contractual performance, gives rise to a category which cannot be subsumed under that of freedom of expression. Hocking calls it "the right to form expectations based on the promises of fellow-men and to depend on their fulfilment." [18]

A man's word is an extension of his person, but once pledged, it is no longer his possession: rather it becomes the property of the one to whom it has been given, and an extension of the person of the latter. Thus a false or broken pledge constitutes a species of predation. The expression, "to *break* one's word," is itself suggestive of an act of violence. At bottom, fraud is but a mode of force.

The very making of a statement (unless it be a conventional civility, or something plainly hyperbolic or manifestly offered in jest) implies that one intends that it be taken as veracious. All serious discourse rests upon the assumption of an implicit contract on the speaker's part to tell the truth, a contract which extends not merely to those to whom one's statements are addressed, but also to those about whom one speaks. Therefore, to falsely defame a person is, in effect, to commit a breach of contract. It also violates the right to property, for a good reputation is a species of incorporeal property which may have a monetary value, or even a value so great as to be beyond price. The bearing of false witness against one's neighbor has from the most ancient times been reprobated, along with theft and murder, as a predatory act. Justice Black's opinion to the contrary notwithstanding, libel and slander are appropriately punishable by law.

*4. The Right to Ownership of Labor Products*   It is astonishing to me how many are seduced by the pompous declaration that "human rights are more important than property rights." Astonishing, because the semantic fallacy on which this silly and mischievous cliché is based is such a glaring one. Not even the most hidebound capitalist has ever held that property as such has rights.* The term "property rights" refers to one of the most fundamental of human rights—the right of human beings to own property.

The right to own property can be readily inferred from the right to freedom of expression. Labor is a form of self-expression: what a man produces is, so to speak, his labor crystallized, and therefore an extension of himself. It is the expenditure of the person in terms of time and effort—the self poured out with varying intensity into so many hours. Therefore, to usurp property legitimately acquired is logically the same as cutting off so many hours from its producer's life, the only difference from murder being that the hours are past instead of future.

The right to property naturally incorporates the rights of gift and bequest, for to deny them is to deny the right of a man to labor voluntarily for others. But it does not incorporate any necessary right to inherit goods apart from the express intention of their owner. Since provision for offspring until they reach maturity is not a matter of mere preference but a solemn obligation assumed in procreation, minor children of one who dies intestate

---

*Objects may have rights, as I suggested near the end of my first chapter, but not in their capacity as property. The rights of property *pertain* to objects but *belong* to men.

have just title to a lien against his assets, as least to the extent of reasonable maintenance during their minority. The just title of a surviving spouse may also be affirmed, although not with the same universality as can the right of minor offspring. But apart from these two exceptions, the latter of which is scarcely absolute, I see no moral reason why the assets of one who dies intestate should not escheat to the public so as to reduce the general burden of supporting the protective structure. It is certainly anything but self-evident that justice requires that an estate automatically devolve upon distant relatives whose very existence may have been unknown to the deceased.

First definitively enunciated by John Locke, the idea that the right to property derives from the right of a man to himself and therefore to his labor, is, I apprehend, no longer academically in vogue. The fashionable approach has for some time now been the "social utility" theory of ownership—the notion that private ownership is only justified if and to the extent that it conduces to the general welfare of society. There have, it is true, been attempts to harmonize the two positions on the ground that "what is best for society is that each man should receive the fruits of his labor." [19] But to say that in the long run justice promotes utility is not the same as saying that utility ought to be the standard for justice. In fact the two theories cannot be reconciled, for each asserts a different norm as ultimate. Yet to accept utility as ultimate is to follow a will-o'-the-wisp, because it always presupposes something else in terms of which it is defined.

The current unpopularity of the labor theory of ownership is partly attributable to the increasing gap between ethics and the social sciences, and to the fact that ethics itself has come to be dominated increasingly by positivists and the devotees of minute linguistic analysis, who recoil with horror at the very mention of the word "rights," believing that it signifies nothing but "metaphysical nonsense," outside the realm of meaningful discussion. Since this belief can hardly hold much weight with any reader who has borne with me thus far, I see no reason to attempt its refutation here. One superficially plausible objection of a more specific nature is, however, frequently adduced, with which it may be apposite to deal.

This is the objection that individual labor never by itself produces anything in civilized society. The very conditions which make civilized production possible result, to be sure, from the contributions of the community. Civilized production depends upon a general fund of knowledge built up through generations of technological experimentation. It depends upon opportunities for marketing, transportation, and the like, which the individual finds already at hand, a legacy from others. It depends upon the materials and the tools he uses, made available by countless men and women the specific identity of most of whom he cannot but be ignorant. All of this is true, but it does not justify the conclusion that the labor theory of ownership should be discarded. This fallacious conclusion, traceable to John Stuart Mill, introduced to the United States by Edward Bellamy, and raised to the sacrosanctity of economic dogma by Edwin R. A. Seligman, amounts to the obvious absurdity that the element of individual labor in production is nonexistent simply because it cannot operate in isolation.

> Take, for example, the workman fashioning a chair. The wood has not been produced by him; it is the gift of nature. The tools that he uses are the results of the contributions of others; the house in which he works, the clothes he wears, the food he eats (all of which are necessary in civilized society to the making of a chair), are the result of the contributions of the community. His safety from robbery and pillage—nay, his very existence—is dependent on the ceaseless cooperation of the society about him. How can it be said, in the face of all this that his own individual labor wholly creates anything? . . . No one has a right to say: This belongs absolutely and completely to me, because I alone have produced it. Society, from this point of view, holds a mortgage on everything that is produced.[20]

Seligman's reasoning really consists of three separate lines of argument, for it is clear that three distinct factors have gone into the making of the chair apart from the contribution of the chairmaker. First, there is the element of natural opportunity represented by the wood. Second, there is the mental and physical labor of other individual producers, signified by the chairmaker's tools, his house, his clothes, his food, etc. Finally, there is his safety from robbery and pillage, guaranteed by government, i.e., by society in its corporate capacity. But unless he is the recipient of special privilege, or his raw material is so abundant as to have no market value, all three of these factors are paid for by the chairmaker with the sweat of his brow, and he owes no further recompense.

> Should he pay twice, once by reimbursing the original owners of these goods and services and then again by turning over a share . . . of his own chairmaking income? It would seem that one payment to society and its members should be morally and practically sufficient.[21]

His ownership of the chair, and of whatever he receives for it, is vindicated by the time and effort he contributed to its production. He alone did not produce it, but without him (or another like him), it would not have been produced. The division of labor creates no mortgage which he has not already satisfied in the ordinary process of exchange. What remains belongs morally to him, free and clear, the just fruit of his toil. It matters not how complex the productive process nor how significant the social contribution: I do not see how this fact can be denied.

An idea is the purest sort of labor product. Having no corporeal embodiment as such, it requires no raw material. It is therefore especially appropriate that the ownership of ideas should be secured to their creators by means of copyright and patent. This is sometimes questioned because mental production draws upon the general stock of cultural and technological attainment, and is therefore never wholly individual. But the use of this deposit is denied to none thereby; in drawing upon it the mental producer does not diminish it but rather brings to it a new element, the touch of his originality, so as to fashion something peculiarly his own.

It is true that the discoverer of a scientific principle or the inventor of a machine but bares to light potential which another might in time reveal. Independent investigators often reach the same conclusions almost simultaneously. For this reason inventions and discoveries are not morally susceptible to ownership in perpetuity, any more than a virgin continent is morally susceptible to the perpetual ownership of one who first sets foot upon it. Thus equity demands limitation of the period for which the protection of a patent should extend. The duration of this period can only be established empirically, by considering "the intervals of time commonly elapsing between similar or identical inventions [or discoveries] made by different men," [22] and even then, approximate justice is the best that can be expected in any given case. The difficulty of specifying its duration with exactitude does not, however, militate against the right of discoverers or inventors to protection.

The above qualification, although customarily applied to it in practice, is not logically or ethically germane to the type of ownership secured by copyright. A literary, artistic, or musical composition is essentially a creation, not a discovery. Theoretically, of course, *War and Peace* or "The Night Watch" might be eventually produced by relays of monkeys pounding typewriters or wielding paintbrushes for millenia, but the independent duplication of a really creative work is so improbable as to be a nugatory consideration. Hence the ownership of mental products of this sort ought to be secured indefinitely.

*5. The Right to Freedom in the Use of Nature*  This right, which Hocking discusses under a similar heading,[23] was never more cogently elucidated than in the original edition of Herbert Spencer's *Social Statics,* where that later agnostic went so far as to speak of it as part of the

"Divine scheme," and where he somewhat crudely anticipated the system of land tenure popularly associated with
the name of Henry George:

> Given a race of beings having like claims to pursue the
> objects of their desires . . . , and it unavoidably follows
> that they have equal rights to the use of this world. For
> if each of them "has freedom to do all that he wills,
> provided he infringes not the equal freedom of any
> other," then each of them is free to use the earth for the
> satisfaction of his wants, provided he allows all others
> the same liberty. And conversely, it is manifest that no
> one, or part of them, may use the earth in such a way
> as to prevent the rest from similarly using it; seeing that
> to do this is to assume greater freedom than the rest, and
> consequently to break the law.[24]

(It is regrettable that the author of this bold statement
came to hedge it about, in his jaundiced and apathetic
old age, with so many fancied barriers to application that
he almost seemed to have abandoned it in principle. It
is no less regrettable that George's magnificent intellectual demolition of these fancied barriers should have
been interwoven with an ill-conceived attack on Spencer's
personal integrity.[25])

From Spencer's formulation, it may be seen that the
right to freedom in the use of nature is not a right to
natural goods themselves so much as an inference from
the law of mutual freedom, which is violated whenever
anyone arrogates to himself exclusive title to their use.
Thus absolute private ownership of land and natural
resources cannot be admitted as a right. They were not
created by human labor, although the mixing of labor
with them may establish a kind of equity in them. But as
we learn from Locke, this equity is qualified by the proviso that there be "enough, and as good left in common
for others" [26] which, translated into economic terms,
means as long as they have no market value. If one accepts
the labor theory of ownership (and I do not know of any
other really fundamental argument for private property),

one is bound to conclude not only that absolute private property in land and natural resources cannot be justified thereby, but that it violates the only kind of property which can. "As labor cannot produce without the use of land, the denial of the equal right to the use of land is necessarily the denial of the right of labor to its own produce." [27] He who would defend the private monopolization of the globe is no more a champion of the true right of property than is he who would defend a robber's title to his booty. The real champion of private ownership must also be the nemesis of spurious ownership. And regardless of how innocently bought and sold, how toilsomely acquired, or how ancient its pedigree, every existing land title will be found to be spurious if traced to its origin. For no king ever had a moral right to legalize the spoil of conquest; no legislature a right to alienate the patrimony of a nation; and no court a right to vest perpetually in any family that which the Creator made for all.

The position just asserted would superficially appear to be incompatible with the principle of territorial sovereignty, an objection urged with skill by the great Lecky:

> If the land of the world is the inalienable possession of the whole human race, no nation has any right to claim one portion of it to the exclusion of the rest. The French have no more right to the soil of France than the Germans. . . . And what possible right, on the principle of Mr. George, have the younger nations to claim for themselves the exclusive possession of vast tracts of fertile and almost uninhabited land, as against the teeming millions of the overcrowded centres of the old world? [28]

Should this objection be sustained, it still would not constitute an admission that the inhabitants of poorer nations necessarily have a moral lien upon the wealth of richer ones. For national prosperity is not alone a matter of favorable climate and location, fertile soil, or abundant natural resources: it depends still more upon good government and the preponderance of such valuable human qualities as creativity, industry, and thrift. And while the application of Lecky's argument might give every Mauritanian Bedouin and Albanian peasant a moral share in the wheatlands of Kansas, it would also give every Swiss banker and Scottish shipbuilder a moral share in the oil fields of Iran. Lecky's objection, however, possesses only prima facie validity. That is to say, it would be valid if all mankind were a single covenant community in which respect for rights were everywhere and equally implanted. Since this is not and will not be foreseeably the case, the covenant community, where it exists, can only protect itself from dissolution by insisting upon territorial sovereignty. In doing this it does not trench upon the universal right to freedom in the use of the earth, so long as it makes membership in the community available to all who will accept its obligations and are not apt to threaten its existence. If the inhabitants of poorer regions are not arbitrarily excluded from immigration, their right is accorded the fullest posssible recognition consistent with the geographically-uneven social progress of the race.

To effectuate the right of equal freedom in the use of nature it is not necessary that all fences be removed and all lands incorporated into one vast commons. It is not necessary that a nation's territory be divided into discrete plots of comparable worth, one for each inhabitant. It is not necessary that private titles be abolished in favor of state ownership. All that is necessary is that those who enjoy the privilege of exclusive tenure indemnify those who are thereby dispossessed. Inasmuch as the annual market value of a site (exclusive of improvements) measures exactly the disadvantage sustained by those who are denied its use, it also measures the amount of just indemnity which any title-holder should be required to pay for his advantage. This indemnity could go into the public treasury to defray protective costs which would otherwise be charged against the fruits of private effort. The social appropriation of site-values would make it economically unprofitable to hold land out of use for purpose of speculation. Rather than having, as at present, to pay a monopolistically inflated price for access to natural opportunity, anyone desiring the secure and private tenure of a site need only pay its use value, as determined by a market rendered truly free. And this payment, instead of being, as at present, a virtual tribute to someone who did nothing to produce that value, would merely be a fair return to those who would otherwise be put at a disadvantage by exclusive tenure, and to the community without whose presence the value of the site would not exist.

This "simple and sovereign remedy" is not a pipe dream. While it has nowhere been applied in toto, it has had sufficient application to confound the dire predictions of its adversaries and to vindicate the commendations of its friends. A discussion of its economic ramifications and administrative aspects would lead us into a technical excursis which has no place within this essay's scope. But years of study have satisfied me that it works. My only object here has been to demonstrate that it is just.

• • •

Where persons or classes of persons are incapable by definition of claiming their just rights, public authority must act for them by enforcing the claims which they could be presumed to make if they were able. Incumbent upon government is the solemn obligation of acting as guardian of the rights of minors, the mentally incompetent and the unborn.*

The act of procreation involves an implicit contract to provide for the sustention of its issue, together with such aids and opportunities as are needed to prepare the latter for self-sufficient adult life. But it should be noted

---

*It also has an obligation to guard the rights of animals and even of inanimate objects, but the limitations of my topic permit me to do no more than note this fact.

that this constitutes a claim upon parents and not upon society at large. Hence the duty of the state is not to provide these goods, but only to enforce the obligation of parents to do so. Lest it be objected that some parents are without financial ability to so provide, this in no way alters the extent of the state's responsibility, any more than financial inability on the part of a divorced spouse makes the payment of alimony incumbent on the state.

Let this be said without equivocation: procreation is no exception to the rule that all rights become void when severed from their concomitant responsibilities. Bringing children into being is a right only for those who are in a position to accept the obligations it entails. Justice demands not that the obligations of the indigent be foisted onto others, but that the indigent be prevented from assuming obligations which they manifestly cannot meet. Medical science has devised techniques which render such prevention possible; that well-meaning people react with horror to the suggestion that their use be made compulsory reflects the power of sentimentality and dogma over the public mind as compared to that of justice. Gilbert Slater remarks that

> to impose existence on a human being is a serious matter; no one has a right to do so without fully resolving to do what can be done in order to secure that such existence is neither miserable in itself nor a cause of injury to the community.[29]

It is idle, however, to trust to conscientious resolutions in this matter: the ones who most require their guidance seldom take thought to make them in the first place, and when they do, are least capable of abiding by them. It is perhaps worthy of mention that Mill's *On Liberty,* one of the most uncompromising of all pleas for the absolute freedom of the individual from unwarranted government interference, contains a passage which powerfully upholds the legitimacy of government action to prevent irresponsible procreation.[30]

What I have said about the indigent applies with even

greater force to carriers of defective genes. In an article entitled "Some Cases Have Right Not To Be Born," a wise and compassionate doctor, formerly of the Mayo Clinic, gives eloquent voice to the plea of an embryo in the womb of an insane woman:

> I very much don't want to be born. I don't want to be brought up in an orphanage, and then be compelled to live all my days as a nameless and utterly lonely and ashamed illegitimate child. I do not want to run the good chance that I will have to live out my days in a mental hospital.[31]

The very conception of this unfortunate was a violation of its rights, which the state had a clear duty to prevent if possible, and, failing that, a duty to prevent its birth.

As trustee of the rights of the unborn, the state is bound to protect them not only against irresponsible parenthood but also against the predatory tendencies of society at large—tendencies of which it has itself been all too often the implementing agent. For the rights of the unborn are not exhausted by the right not to be born of those for whom birth would be a cruel offense, but include as well the natural and social legacy upon which general posterity has an indefeasible claim. Nature and freedom together constitute an entailed estate, the principal of which no generation may legitimately squander.

The state does fulfill to some extent its obligation in the conservation of certain natural resources which have not already been monopolized and despoiled with its assistance. But while the conservation of nature is thus feebly undertaken, the conservation of freedom is increasingly more honored in the breach than the observance. When present prosperity is purchased at a price which will hang like a millstone around the neck of future generations, a gross betrayal of stewardship has been committed. Deficit spending for national defense may be defended when it is the only means whereby free institutions can be preserved as a heritage for citizens yet to come. Deficit spending to maintain fat living standards at posterity's expense is morally indefensible, especially when perpetrated by that very agency which is mandated with the task of seeing to it that posterity's rights are kept inviolate.

There is one sense in which Rousseau was right about "forcing people to be free." Freedom is an inalienable trust. Nobody has the right to opt for any form of servitude which is likely to extend beyond the one who does the opting. This means that a just constitution can never leave the door open for the people, in their corporate capacity, to barter freedom for welfare. When majority rule is unrestrained as the supreme political principle of a nation's fundamental law, the course of history attests that this is exactly what they will do.

> Is it just or reasonable, that most voices against the main end of government should enslave the less number that would be free? More just it is, doubtless, if it come to force, that a less number compel a greater to retain, which can be no wrong to them, their liberty, than that a greater number for the pleasure of their baseness, compel a less most injuriously to be their fellow slaves. They who seek nothing but their own just liberty, have always the right to win it, whenever they have the power, be the voices never so numerous that oppose it.[32]

• • •

In my enumeration of the various rights which follow from the primal right of freedom from predation, critics may descry the absence of any reference to "political rights." The omission was not unintentional. Participation in government, whether through the exercise of suffrage or the holding of public office, cannot be considered a right in the sense of being an immediate inference from the principle of reciprocal freedom. It is a conditional duty, built into that machinery which has been found generally most instrumental to the covenant's operation. It is a right only where that machinery is actually most instrumental, and only to those qualified for its performance. To deny someone the vote is not intrinsically a denial of his right to mutual freedom. It is, however, a denial of a power which, if properly used, may help safeguard that right; therefore arbitrary restrictions on the franchise are unjust. Yet because this power may equally be used to trench upon the liberties of others and to undermine the covenant, there is nothing arbitrary in withholding the franchise from those who do not meet certain uniform and rational standards.

Also absent from this catalogue of rights is any mention of freedom of worship, freedom of inquiry, etc. I have not dealt specifically with these, since they are such obvious facets of the right to freedom of expression. Nevertheless it is worthy of comment that because rights of this sort seem to be uniquely related to man's spiritual vocation, certain thinkers, of whom Berdyaev may be taken as a type, would zealously safeguard them while at the same time allowing for drastic encroachment upon other rights. Freedom is dissected, and then reconstituted, according to a kind of graded hierarchy:

> Freedom should increase in measure as it approaches spirit, and decrease as it approaches the material. The greatest freedom is that of spiritual life; the minimum is the freedom of material existence. . . . In the name of freedom itself, economic freedom must be limited. But as we rise from the material to the spiritual side of life, freedom ought to increase. And while it may occasionally be possible to have an economic or political dictatorship, dictatorship in the realm of spirit and of the intellectual is neither permissible nor justifiable.[33]

Yet the precarious state of spiritual and intellectual freedom under any variety of unrestricted domination was realized full well by Berdyaev himself when he raised the following prophetic question:

> Can these dictatorships confine themselves only to politics and economics, or is it inevitable that they also become dictatorships of world-view, of ideas, of the spirit, that is to say, of all free spiritual life and work and conscience?" [34]

There is something pathetic in this query, as if the author knew, even as he wrote, that he was indulging in an extravagant, albeit timid, hope.

It is in the nature of the authoritarian state to encroach upon freedom of the spirit. Berdyaev's segmentation of life according to degree of relationship to matter savors of Gnosticism rather than of Christianity. The more authentically Christian orientation is that of the Fourth Gospel, in which (as H. Richard Niebuhr tells us)

> the physical, material, and temporal are never regarded as participating in evil in any particular way because they are not spiritual and eternal. . . . Spiritual and natural events are "interlocking and analogous." [35]

Freedom is indivisible. Wisely indeed does Wilhelm Röpke comment: "It is hardly forgiveable naïvete to believe that a state can be all-powerful in the economic sphere without also being autocratic in the political and intellectual domain." [36] And sound indeed is the admonition of Lord Acton that "it is only by abridging the authority of states that the liberty of churches can be assured." [37]

# Maintaining The Covenant

In the state of nature rights exist but they are enforceable only in proportion to their claimants' power. Only within the covenant does the enforcement of rights itself become a right. Here the power of the whole supports the rights even of those who can contribute nothing to that power; it does this not out of charity but out of solicitude for the rights themselves.

But those who can contribute and will not, or who repudiate the covenant and oppose their power to its provisions, remove themselves from the beneficent sphere of its protection, and revert to the state of nature, forfeiting the right to have their rights enforced. They become, quite literally, *outlaws.* If, like Thoreau, they merely decline to contribute their share to the power of the whole, they may be left to defend themselves individually against predation as best they can, so long as they present no threat to the community in whose midst they live. If, however, they declare by word or deed aggressive war against the covenant, its adherents have no choice but to treat them as wild beasts to be forcibly restrained or, if need be, eliminated.* Since they are not party to

---

*This judgment applies to nations as well as to individuals.

the compact, they cannot be justly punished for breaking it, any more than a rabid dog can be justly *punished* for sinking its fangs into a child. Retributive justice is germane only against those who violate a mutually understood ideal. But this is not to say that society should not defend itself with measures as severe as may be necessary, or that rabid dogs should not be shot.

The protocols which bind together the "community of concurrence in matters of right" define not only its members' behavior toward each other but also the community's behavior toward its members. These protocols, however, scarcely limit the community's behavior toward those who do not recognize them as authoritative. He who reverts to or remains in the state of nature reserves to himself the privilege of defining his own rights and contending for them in whatever way he chooses. He may expect the community to do the same in its relationship to him.

It is a false analysis which opposes freedom to order. Order is not the contrary of freedom; it is the effective maintenance of its reciprocal distribution. When a meeting is "called to order," the object is not to reduce freedom but to insure that it be reciprocally apportioned— to insure that no one be permitted to monopolize the floor and thereby interfere with the freedom of others to express themselves within the bounds of pertinence and decorum. Non-reciprocal freedom is not true freedom but license. A society where insufficient authority exists to keep freedom reciprocal is not a free society but an anarchic one. Anarchy and privilege are but two forms of the same evil: anarchy is license unrestrained; privilege is license enforced. Both are licentious: the first because authority is too weak to do a job that must be done; the second because authority does precisely that which its job is to prevent.

Just as, for the sake of order, a heavy gavel must be wielded in some meetings, so a strong and active sword must be wielded in some societies. Where traditions of responsible self-government do not obtain, there may be no alternative but to severely restrict the freedom of all so as to guarantee to all a reciprocal measure of freedom. Parliamentary institutions forfeit their prerogatives when they prove too indecisive or too venal for this task. Under such circumstances, in Latin America and elsewhere the military traditionally intervenes in its self-appointed capacity as trustee. That such intervention is repugnant to Anglo-Saxon mores should not obscure the fact that no other viable option may be available. If only a man on horseback is capable of imposing order, freedom is not served by insistence on the niceties of parliamentary democracy. The legitimacy of his authority is vindicated by his power, in the absence of any other, to exercise it. It is perhaps unlikely that he will do so without abuse. Yet a parliamentary body may have amply demonstrated that it lacks *both* the power to enforce order *and* the self-restraint to avoid enforcing privilege.

Similarly, colonial domination, even if historically a tool of privilege, may in some instances provide a better surety of order than native governments, popular or otherwise.[1] But the risks of anarchy and tyranny to which an unprepared population is exposed by premature independence are often outweighed in cost to that population by the sustained harsh measures, themselves fraught with a propensity to menace order, which the deferment of independence usually entails. When this is so, the continuance of colonial rule loses its provisional justification.[2]

Problems such as these must be decided in terms of whatever course of action is situationally most conducive to reciprocal freedom. Whether a parliamentary government too inept to secure order is to be preferred to an autocrat who can secure order but who is also liable to violate it by the misdirected or excessive use of power; whether the continuance of a colonial presence in the face of widespread native opposition is to be preferred to a withdrawal that would leave innocent minorities dependent for protection upon a feeble or unsympathetic new regime—these are questions the answers to which can only rest upon a shrewd assessment of contextual factors in each concrete case. It is here that Fletcher's agapēic calculus comes rightly into play, but with this difference: love's prime desideratum is in every context understood to be the reign of order—the most effective maintenance of reciprocal freedom which, within the circumstances, can be achieved. This desideratum is the universal framework which must be served regardless of the situation; but the means whereby to serve it are relative to the situation and cannot be prescriptively determined in isolation. The defense of the framework is not seldom a grim and necessarily ruthless struggle, in which quarter can be neither asked of nor given to the forces by which order is assailed. It is a struggle in which the most responsible— and therefore the most loving—tactics are not always the mildest and most gentlemanly tactics. "The necessary end sanctifies the necessary means," [3] and reciprocal freedom is an end which hallows any means required for its defense—assuming, of course, that they do not frustrate their object in the long run. Whether this assumption can be made in any given case depends upon the circumstances, and is a matter for prayerful and diligent contextual study and consideration.

Implied in the foregoing discussion is the premise that equal freedom means maximum freedom consistent with equal distribution. The quantity of freedom which is susceptible of equal distribution is not fixed but varies according to the empirical conditions of each case. Yet freedom may be needlessly restricted, even where it is seemingly reciprocally apportioned. This is the fatal joker in Rousseau's social formula. A sovereign (whether autocrat or majority) may accept austerely for itself every limitation it imposes on the whole. But it arrogates to itself an illicit and undue freedom—a kind of Spartan license—whenever it imposes limitations which exceed those requisite to the enforcement of reciprocity.[4]

Although order does not logically or necessarily call for any particular form of governmental structure, the weight of historical evidence rather plainly suggests that order is generally most effectively secured by representative institutions with judicious safeguards against majority tyranny. This is because such a structure best provides for the balancing of interests needed to preclude abuse of power, while at the same time permitting broad enough participation to place the force of public opinion behind policies which bear the stamp of mutual agreement. It moreover allows most fully for the peaceful redress of grievances through processes of legal change, obviating, where it has not been vitiated, against violent civil disorders which are otherwise sometimes vindicated by the absence of alternatives.

There is no special virtue attached to obedience to constituted authority or human law as such. The Declaration of Independence unequivocally asserts that refusal to obey unjust laws or arbitrary rulers can be a duty under certain circumstances, and in this it but reiterates a theme earlier popularized by those sixteenth-century followers of Calvin to whom historians have applied the term "Monarchomachists." Where representative institutions obtain in fact as well as theory, the presumption is that those aggrieved should obey laws and rulers which they deem unjust, since avenues of peaceful change are open to them. But where an entrenched regime is able to perpetuate itself in power by means of the Hopkinsian strategy of "tax, spend, elect," or where it arrogates to itself advantages of propaganda which make a mockery of the processes of consent, methods of persuasion cannot be depended upon to correct abuse, and militant resistance may be justified as a last resort.

• • •

Inasmuch as responsible decisions cannot be expected of an ignorant electorate, education becomes an auxiliary concern of any polity which incorporates a broad-based franchise. This means that the cost of such training as may be deemed essential for informed citizenship is a legitimate public charge. The taxpayer has no moral duty to subsidize either the aesthetic cultivation or the vocational preparation of the young; such subsidy is a parental responsibility. His just obligation is limited to the support of necessary education for citizenship. Little of what goes on in most schools, especially public ones, has any clear relationship to this goal. Responsible exercise of the franchise would seem to require that a voter be able to read easily, think logically, and have some basic knowledge of economics, history, and political institutions. Yet vast numbers of young people spend their time in school being titillated at public expense by courses in music appreciation, woodworking, and tennis, and then go out into the world without ever having learned to read anything more demanding than the comics. Logic is never and economics seldom offered below the college level, and history and civics are more often than not relegated to be taught by physical education personnel whose lack of academic background in the subjects is exceeded only by their lack of interest in them. Is it any wonder that the average voter is politically naive and readily seduced?

Effective education for citizenship demands not merely that youth be drilled in civic facts and taught the fundamentals of valid reasoning. It demands, above all else, the cultivation of an attitude of dedication to the covenant, and of respect for the principles and institutions whereby the covenant is actualized. This is to assert that effective education for citizenship is essentially a matter of moral indoctrination. But government, even on a local level, is the worst possible instrument with which to undertake this task.

To say that education for citizenship should be publicly supported is not to say that schools should be publicly operated. As Mill long ago warned, publicly operated education is vulnerable to perversion as a vehicle for partisan influence;[5] even Jefferson sought to make of the University of Virginia such a vehicle.[6] "The more highly one rates the power that education can have over men's minds, the more convinced one should be of the danger of placing this power in the hands of any single authority." [7] Since the natural tendency of government is to expand its scope, how can it be safely entrusted with the responsibility of operating schools which have as their main purpose the inculcation of reverence for a covenant which incorporates the concept that the legitimate scope of government is sharply limited?

Even if the foregoing objection did not obtain, there is an equally compelling reason why schools should not be publicly operated. While the propensity of government to overstep its bounds makes public education liable to misuse as an engine of statist propaganda, any political agency which really sought to keep within its proper sphere would be rendered by its very conscientiousness incapable of educating effectively for citizenship. For to be effective, education must be radical—radical in the sense of starting from the roots of its objective. The roots of the covenant are religious. Severed from them, it withers like a cut flower. But the idea of equality before the law prohibits the state from acting as an affirmative preceptor of religion.

The bond of the covenant community is reciprocal freedom, the primal right of which all others are particularizations. The covenant embraces all who claim this right and accept its concomitant responsibilities, regardless of whether their motives be humanistic, utilitarian, or theocentric. It thus envisages a pluralistic order, and for this reason cannot authorize any kind of official religious establishment, however broad. Yet, as I endeavored to show in my prolegomena, freedom can ultimately be justified only by a theocentric rationale, and unless the covenant is undergirded by a theocentric commitment it cannot stand. The inculcation of such a commitment by the state is precluded by the heterogeneity of its constituency. Because of this heterogeneity, the state can only undertake such moral indoctrination as may be acceptable to the lowest common denominator, and which is bound, therefore, to be thin, superficial, and hence ineffectual.

It is thus upon the private school that the mission of training citizens best devolves, for only it can be free to orient that training to the spiritual end which gives it its final meaning and sanction. Such training is required by the general public interest as essential to the functioning of representative institutions, and its support is, therefore, a proper public charge. Several nations and other political entities permit the individual taxpayer (or parent, as the case may be) to designate a non-public system of his choice as recipient of his share of the public educational expenditure, the role of government being limited, when this occurs, to the collection of such funds and the enforcement of minimum academic standards. Milton Friedman has advocated the adoption of this approach in the United States in lieu of government-operated schools,[8] and Hayek endorses it as being now "entirely practicable" in view of various social and technological advances which militate against objections that might once have been conclusive.[9] Under such an approach, needless to say, secular and even atheistic schools could not equitably be denied the tax support of their sympathizers. But those who trace the covenant's authority to a divine mandate would have freedom to make that mandate the cornerstone of their educational projects without being at the same time forced, as at present, to underwrite the cost of education which is secular and statist.

· · ·

The only equality compatible *with* liberty is that equality *of* liberty which is essential to keep liberty from degenerating into license. The two principles are otherwise mutually repugnant. Equality in any other sense will crush out freedom, reducing society to a dead level of uniformity which has no functional warrant. This is why "equality before the law" does not mean that the law should be used to make people equal, but rather that it should treat them with impartiality in its capacity as guarantor of their equal right to freedom. Any attempt by law to make them equal in condition would be a perversion of the law's office, as it would necessitate discrimination on behalf of some at the expense of others.[10]

As for "equality of opportunity" in the full, literal meaning of the term, it, too, can be implemented only by means of inequality before the law. If government seriously undertakes to enforce equality of opportunity, it must go beyond preventing predation and the unequal advantages which arise therefrom, and seek to redress inequalities resulting from differences in native endowment. It can only do this by conferring special privileges on some of the expense of others, or by instituting artificial handicaps which penalize favorable heredity. The enforcement of equal *freedom* of opportunity, on the other hand, is a legitimate and essential function of public authority—a function which is not merely compatible with but which is required by the ideal of equality before the law. The organs of government in a free commonwealth can have no more imperative duty than to prevent the coercive monopolization of opportunity, and to extirpate it where it obtains.* The extent to which such

---

*The propriety of such a duty in terms of libertarian theory is recognized by none other than Bertrand de Jouvenel, who writes: "Social arrangements may be such as to introduce inequalities which are not the natural result of the process of creation of resources. This is what happens when social elements allot themselves, or get themselves allotted, important blocks of resources either because of the power they wield or in consideration of services which are thought to render but do not render—or no longer render effectively. This is the phenomenon to which the word 'exploitation' is properly applicable. . . . This phenomenon has played a large part in social history, where the inequalities created by it tend to be perpetuated almost indefinitely when the resulting privileged positions have taken the form of concrete rights over natural resources. Thus we see that rights created in the Middle Ages have governed down to our time the possession of certain lands on which stands the City of

coercive monopolization has been sanctioned, encouraged, and effected by the American government ever since its founding is some indication of how far from being a free commonwealth our nation really is.

The principle of equality before the law, however, raises certain problems of interpretation, both in terms of legal process and of public costs. Granting that justice does not signify the equalizing of conditions, unequal conditions must not be permitted to interfere with its availability to all who stand within the covenant community. A man's ability to pay should have no bearing upon his eligibility to receive the benefits of law. Our juristic arrangements reflect a dim apprehension of this insight by providing, at public expense, counsel for indigent defendants. How dim an apprehension is suggested by the fact that such counsel is usually inexperienced, and invariably overworked and underpaid, not to mention the fact that no provision at all is ordinarily made for cases in equity. Serious consideration needs to be given to the question of whether, if equality before the law is to be other than a farce, private wealth should be allowed to purchase legal representation or advice superior, in either quality or quantity, to that which is available to the meanest pauper.*

In the area of public revenue the principle of equality before the law gives rise to issues especially subtle and complex. Where a man abstracts from the common store

---

London. The example evokes the possibility of like efforts resulting from the direct appropriation of natural resources, as in the case of the land on which Manhattan stands. Here we have causes of inequalities of a non-structural kind, in which the intervention of authority is not illegitimate" (*Sovereignty*, trans. J. F. Huntington, Chicago: University of Chicago Press, 1957, p. 162n).

*Since the fundamental purpose of government is justice, this line of reasoning is germane to the entire political process—not merely to law in the narrow sense of the term, i.e., pertaining to the business of courts and attorneys. For this reason I believe that there is merit in the proposal that all electioneering costs be met by public subsidy, and that no candidate be permitted to draw upon private wealth for campaign purposes.

of opportunity some good which is thereby denied to others, it seems clear that he should pay the community the full value of his special advantage. The benefit theory of taxation is thus applicable to public revenues derived from ground rent, rent for airwaves, and severance taxes on natural resources. The benefit theory is also applicable in cases where a public service is provided not as a matter of compulsion but of convenience to the voluntary user. Insofar as roads and highways are maintained for purposes other than defense, gasoline taxes and toll fees fall into this category, as do parking meter fees, which are further justified as a species of ground rent. None of the above, however, can be classified as true taxes, but are rather public fees.

The benefit theory is less germane to special assessments, as for paving and sewage, for even though the proportionate costs of such benefits are determinate, the benefits are provided without reference to individual option. This seems to me a persuasive argument against the public provision of services which are not voluntarily accepted by all users, and which are not vital to the general health and safety or the functioning of necessary institutional machinery. Where services such as sewage, lighting, garbage collection, etc. are publicly provided on grounds of general protection, the benefit theory does not apply, and the case for special assessment gives way to the case for a more general levy. Where such services cannot be justified on general protective grounds, neither can compulsory support be justified, regardless of the manner in which that support may be apportioned.

Sidgwick has acutely stated the reason why the benefit theory is not apposite to the support of general protective functions—i.e., to the support of government activities addressed to the maintenance of rights:

> Nor does it seem that there is necessarily any sacrifice of justice, even from an individualistic point of view, in throwing a part of the cost of services which men are compelled to purchase on persons other than the reci-

pient; since from this point of view the only admissible reason for compelling any individual to purchase such services is that the interests of others will be damaged if he is allowed to dispense with them; hence it seems not unfair that others should bear a part of their cost.[11]

There is indeed "benefit received" at issue here; however, that which is conclusive is not the direct positive benefit to the individual but the indirect negative benefit to the community, and when this complication is introduced, the rule that each person should pay according to benefit becomes useless as a guide. If the benefit theory is thus abandoned, we are obliged to consider other theoretical bases for the distribution of the tax burden. Foremost among these is the theory of ability to pay, expressed in practice by the method of progressive rates. Insofar as this theory rests upon no deeper rationale, it may be dismissed immediately as morally obnoxious, as it nowise differs from the logic of the brigand whose choice among prospective victims depends upon the respective fatness of their purses. Ability to pay, however, has also been regarded as a measure of equal sacrifice, and on this ground presents an ostensibly more respectable claim. Yet specialists in public revenue theory are by no means in agreement as to what is really meant by equal sacrifice, or that it is actually best measured by progressive rates determined by ability.[12] Indeed the whole idea of equal sacrifice appears, when subjected to marginal utility analysis, too subjective to admit of that quantification requisite to its meaningful application to the distribution of public fiscal burdens. A free market can measure the marginal utility of relative satisfactions and therefore sacrifices as among its participants, but since taxes, being compulsory, do not reflect a market situation, it is difficult to see how they can be apportioned in terms of equal sacrifice.

In view of these complications some thinkers would assess the justice of a tax system solely in terms of the system's efficacy in meeting broad social needs, without reference to its relative burden upon individual taxpayers except as that burden may have public consequences. Yet it would be hard to name, even on utilitarian grounds, any social need (save possibly sheer survival) which can take precedence over equality before the law, which is, after all, imperative to the very fabric of a rational social order. For this reason the question of relative individual burden cannot be put aside.

The entire problem of apportioning the tax burden would be obviated if we could assume, as Henry George assumed with reason in his day, that indemnities for special advantages abstracted from the common stock of natural opportunity would, if set at the full market value of such advantages, be sufficient to defray the total cost of government's essential functions. Even in the light of today's expanded military budgets, this assumption need not be laughed out of court. Insofar as monopolistic privilege begets social evils which give rise to public expense, the indemnities, to the extent that they would extirpate such privilege, would concurrently reduce the need for public revenue. Furthermore, there is substantial evidence that the potential ground rent fund is a great deal larger than is commonly supposed.[13] Even if there should still remain the problem of apportioning the difference, it seems both practicable and fair that this approach be used as far as it will go. The total fund of rent for natural opportunity, divided by the number of persons having an equal right to government protection, would give a figure representing the amount in which each person might be equitably exempted from taxation. As for the balance which might yet need to be collected, and which could be presumed to signify the cost of protecting property instead of persons*, it seems to me that

---

*There is, of course, actually no way of separating these two kinds of protection in terms of cost, yet the above proposition is nonetheless not arbitrary. It rests upon the proposition that, so far as possible, free protection be extended equally to everyone, and that beyond this point, protective costs be distributed according to the amount of wealth a person has to be protected.

rates should be proportionate rather than prog essive. I say this because the benefit theory, while inapplicable to the protection of persons, has at least some relevance to that of property, inasmuch as, while no one who is part of the covenant community can decline to be included within the sphere of its protective service, an individual is at liberty to reduce his property or income to the amount on which he is willing to pay protective charges. Objective benefit is measured by the multiple of units of economic value which enjoy protection, and this results in a proportionate rate. Could subjective benefit be quantified, it would lead to a regressive schedule since the marginal utility of wealth for its possessor is highest at the bottom.

If the issue of taxation presents difficulties in terms of the principle of equality before the law, the issue of military service presents ones still more formidable. The conscription of dollars has to do with units which are at least objectively commensurable, even though perhaps they cannot be equated from the standpoint of subjective valuation. The conscription of service has to do with units which are qualitatively unlike, and which thus defy correlation altogether.* The very term *"selective service"* suggests something alien to the idea of equal treatment. It may, of course, be said that all are equally liable to serve, and that "selection" is based on military need rather than on favoritism. Yet equal liability is but a formal norm: in practice, the conscription of service is inherently discriminatory. Even if the draft be extended to cover all legally competent adults, its object would be defeated or, at any rate seriously hindered, were all assigned to duty of like hazard and rigor.

The fairest way to apportion the compulsory burden of defense is to do so by taxation, using revenue thus obtained to pay whatever price is necessary to induce the required number of men to engage in service on a volun-

---

*This objection does not apply to jury duty, which imposes an objectively identical form of service upon all who are conscripted.

tary basis. In view of the increasingly sophisticated nature of modern warfare, there is strong reason to believe that an armed force made up of well-paid, highly-qualified careerists would be both more efficient and more economical than the present wasteful policy of training vast hordes of men conscripted for relatively short-term periods, whose entry into military life is motivated neither by aptitude nor by enthusiasm. It may be that in the face of an extraordinary threat the requirements for survival should outweigh the importance of equality before the law, and recourse be had to the method of compulsory service. Yet, assuming inducements competitive to those of other occupations of like danger, if a sufficient number of military personnel cannot be obtained through voluntary means, this places under grave suspicion the legitimacy of the military purpose for which their service is required. There is a weighty presumption against any cause for which men will not come forward willingly to take up arms.

While the compulsory performance of military service cannot be unambiguously deduced, as can the payment of taxes, from the duty to support the protective operation of the covenant, there is another type of service which this duty imposes in equal measure upon all who find themselves in circumstances which call forth its exercise. One who remains passive when aware of crime is rightly regarded as an accessory. When the official agencies of society neglect their protective functions or are prevented by ignorance or situational exigencies from fulfilling them, the obligation to defend the innocent devolves in a direct and personal way upon the individual. This is why criminal culpability may be assigned to the neighbors who stood by and watched the sadistic rape-murder of Kitty Genovese without intervening even to the extent of calling the authorities. Their duty was not so much to the pathetic victim herself as to the covenant under which their common safety was presumptively assured. As Lord Bryce observes, there are even situations where lynch law represents, in the absence of effectively functioning official organs, the only way in which the protective office of the covenant can be given real expression.[14]

• • •

The national state, insofar as it embodies the community of covenant, does so but parochially; the covenant, it will be recalled, is the *universal* framework of conditions under which men are capable of sustained voluntary interrelationship—the mutually understood ideal without which there can be no peace save for the brutal equilibrium of raw, amoral power. Taylor, from whom I have borrowed the term, uses it to signify the "articles" or "rules of the game" which are requisite to all sustained free association, political or otherwise. In economics, for example, it is that tissue of reciprocal assumptions which transmutes competition from the practice of the jungle to a phase of that great cooperative endeavor we call the market. In the realm of intellect it is the acceptance of common principles of evidence as normative for rational discourse. In the realm of art it is the acknowledgment of canons whereby works may be objectively evaluated.

The obligation to support the covenant devolves, then, upon nations as well as upon individuals. It is palpably incompatible with the concept of unrestricted sovereignty, which cannot be accommodated to respect for international law. Yet sovereignty, as a locus of absolute authority, is, when attached to supra-national organs, no less inadmissible and still more to be feared. Only a Hobbesian should be willing to exchange the anarchy of competing national sovereignties for the leviathan of a world sovereignty. If such be the price of peace, better the risk of mutual annihilation, for there is neither counterweight to nor refuge from the tyranny of a world leviathan.

It would be reassuring were we able to discern, as many do, the lineaments of the universal covenant community in the United Nations or some other existing supra-national structure. The most promising movement toward the supra-national materialization of the covenant seemed to be the organization of free trade and travel areas, most notably the European Common Market. Yet in the light of the Christian view of man, it should be no occasion for surprise that even this apparently hopeful development has in practice turned out to be a mere consolidation of barriers and controls. Some degree of confidence appears to be invited by the performance of the World Court. But one wonders if the encouraging restraint of that performance does not simply reflect extremely modest jurisdiction and the absence of enforcement apparatus. If power corrupts, the lack of it may well produce the illusion of incorruptibility! As for the United Nations, even its impotence has not delivered it from irresponsible and grandiose pretensions, however much that impotence may provide a safeguard against their effectuation. In some few places the covenant community has found incipient concretion on national levels. While no one who is not grossly self-deluded can imagine this concretion to be other than imperfect, it nonetheless represents the highest political advance which fallen humanity has yet achieved. These oases of relative justice are far outnumbered in the United Nations by states which have exhibited little evidence of being significantly influenced by the ideal of reciprocal freedom. It is well that the covenant community, where partly actualized, is not as yet materially subject to a collective will which cannot but be alien to it. The very fact that the United Nations would adopt anything so absurd as its Universal Declaration of Human Rights is proof of its untrustworthiness to wield supreme authority. Reciprocal freedom has nothing to do with such vain and demagogic follies as the demand that everyone, as a matter of right, be accorded "periodic holidays with pay." [15] If the United Nations had the power to enforce its declaration, we should see the sacrifice of genuine rights to spurious ones.

Not until the covenant is *internally* embraced can it

become the basis of an authentic world community, and it would be utopian to predict that this will ever happen temporally on anything approaching a total scale. The thing most necessary is to maintain and nourish it where it does exist, instead of permitting it to be engulfed and ultimately extinguished by a counterfeit. We dare not hope that in the tainted and unredeemed sphere of history it will be actualized as a truly universal order. But we can expect that it will at least find wider rootage in the hearts of men if those peoples in whose institutions it has been given relative expression preserve and perfect that expression as an example to the world, guarding vigilantly *for its sake* the integrity of their independence. For the national state is functionally justified only as it serves the covenant.

Yet the covenant, the ultimate political criterion, is not intrinsically authoritative. It is authoritative, rather, because it serves in turn a higher covenant not of this earth. It draws no vitality from veneration as an idol but solely from use as an instrument, an instrument consecrated not to human wants but to divine will. Upon our recapture and reaffirmation of this truth may rest the possibility not merely of its growth but indeed of its survival. Upon our recapture and reaffirmation of this truth does rest our corporate salvation as a nation under God.

# Notes

## Prolegomena

1. "Conflict of Values: Freedom and Justice," in *Goals of Economic Life*, ed. Dudley A. Ward (New York: Harper, 1953), p. 205.

2. See Richard B. Brandt, ed., *Social Justice* (Englewood Cliffs, N. J.: Prentice-Hall, 1962), p. v.

3. Plato, *The Republic*, Bk. 1.

4. *The Ego and His Own*, trans. S. T. Byington, Modern Library ed. (New York: Boni and Liveright, 1912), p. 218.

5. James Bryce, *The American Commonwealth*, 2nd ed. (London: Macmillan, 1891), I, 299.

6. Charles Grove Haines, *The Revival of Natural Law Concepts* (Cambridge: Harvard University Press, 1930), p. 340.

7. *Religion and the Social Problem* (Philadelphia: Intercollegiate Society of Individualists, 1956), p. 12.

8. Jean-Jacques Rousseau, *The Social Contract and Discourses*, trans. G. D. H. Cole, Everyman's Library ed. (London: Dent, 1947), pp. 3, 12.

9. *Introduction to Social Contract: Essays by Locke, Hume, and Rousseau* (New York: Oxford University Press, 1948), pp. xxxiv–xxxv.

10. Rousseau, *The Social Contract and Discourses*, p. 15.

11. John E. E. D. Acton, *Essays on Freedom and Power* (Boston: Beacon Press, 1948), p. 12.

12. Jacques Maritain, *The Rights of Man and Natural Law* (New York: Scribners, 1943), pp. 65–68.

*13.* John 11:50, 18:14. Except where otherwise indicated all scripture references are to the Revised Standard Version of the Bible.

*14. An Inquiry Into the Original of Our Ideas of Beauty and Virtue,* 3rd ed. (London: J. and J. Knapton et al., 1729), pp. 179–180.

*15.* John Bowring, ed., *The Works of Jeremy Bentham* (Edinburgh: Tait, 1838–43), IV, 122.

*16. American Democracy and Natural Law* (New York: Columbia University Press, 1950), p. 13.

*17.* Ibid., p. 100.

*18.* Ibid., p. 135.

*19.* See Emil Brunner, *The Divine Imperative,* trans. Olive Wyon (London: Lutterworth Press, 1937), pp. 295–307.

*20.* Maritain, *The Rights of Man and Natural Law,* pp. 65–68.

*21. Summa Theologica,* 1, q. 95, a. 1.

*22. An Interpretation of Christian Ethics* (New York: Harper, 1935), p. 32.

*23.* Quoted in Emil Brunner, *Justice and the Social Order,* trans. Mary Hottinger (New York: Harper, 1945), p. 268.

*24.* Ibid., p. 281. In context (Luther's treatise "On Marriage Matters") the statement actually has reference to law in the narrow sense rather than to justice, and *Recht* is so translated in the definitive American edition of Luther's works (Philadelphia: Fortress Press, 1967, XLVI, 289). Even though the Brunner-Hottinger rendering is somewhat misleading with respect to Luther's specific meaning in the marriage treatise, I feel justified in using it as faithfully expressive of the general tenor of his thought.

For a detailed technical study of the morphology of Luther's social concepts, see F. Edward Cranz, *An Essay on the Development of Luther's Thought on Justice, Law, and Society,* Harvard Theological Studies, XIX (Cambridge: Harvard University Press, 1959).

*25. Lectures on Calvinism,* delivered at Princeton Theological Seminary on the L. P. Stone Foundation (New York: Fleming H. Revell Company, 1898), pp. 126–127.

*26.* See Brunner, *Justice and the Social Order,* p. 267.

*27. Commentary on Genesis,* 8:21.

*28.* T. F. Torrance, *Calvin's Doctrine of Man* (London: Lutterworth Press, 1949), pp. 66, 110.

*29. Institutes of the Christian Religion,* Bk. III, Chap. XIV, Sec. 2.

*30.* Torrance, *Calvin's Doctrine of Man,* p. 93.

*31. Commentaries on the First Book of Moses Called Genesis* (Edinburgh: Calvin Translation Society, 1847), I, 295–296.

*32. Institutes,* Bk. III, Chap. VII, Sec. 6.

*33.* See Martin Luther, "Secular Authority: To What Extent It Should Be Obeyed," in *Works* (Philadelphia: Muhlenberg Press, 1943), III, 24–25.

*34. Justice and the Social Order,* p. 266.

*35. Institutes,* Bk. IV, Chap. XX.

*36.* Torrance, *Calvin's Doctrine of Man,* p. 93.

*37.* Ibid., p. 58.

*38.* Ibid., pp. 65–66.

*39.* Ernst Troeltsch, *The Social Teaching of the Christian Churches,* trans. Olive Wyon (London: George Allen & Unwin, 1931), II, 589.

*40.* See his letter to Bucer, *Corpus Reformatorum,* ed. Guilielmus Baum et al. (Brunswick, 1863), XXIX, 883 ff.

*41.* Troeltsch, *The Social Teaching of the Christian Churches,* II, 506.

*42.* See Max Weber, *The Protestant Ethic and the Spirit of Capitalism,* trans. Talcott Parsons (New York: Scribners, 1930), p. 109.

*43. The Social Teaching of the Christian Churches,* II, 621.

*44.* "Prophet of Man's Glory and Tragedy," *New York Times Book Review,* January 29, 1956, pp. 6–7.

*45.* See Brunner, *The Divine Imperative,* pp. 663, 665.

## Chapter One

*1.* Charles Frankel, ed., *The Uses of Philosophy: An Irwin Edman Reader* (New York: Simon and Schuster, 1955), p. 27.

*2. Kant's Critique of Practical Reason and Other Works on the Theory of Ethics,* trans. T. K. Abbot (London: Longmans, Green, 1873), p. 243 and passim.

*3. Foundations of the Metaphysic of Morals,* First Sec., par. 1.

*4.* The passages are summarized in Norman Kemp Smith, *Commentary to Kant's Critique of Pure Reason,* 2nd ed. (London: Macmillian, 1923), Appendix C.

*5. The Source of Human Good* (Chicago: University of Chicago Press, 1946), p. 267.

6. *Religion Within the Limits of Reason Alone,* Bk. II, Sec. 1, Pt. C.

7. I Corinthians 7:31 (Authorized Version).

8. *Natural Rights* (London: George Allen & Unwin, 1894), p. 108. See also p. 61 (n. 2), in which Ritchie, through levity, misses the whole point of J. Lorrimer's reference in his *Institutes of Law* to the "rights of the last rose of summer not to be plucked." For a devastating critique of Ritchie's book, see Francis Neilson, *The Eleventh Commandment* (New York: Viking Press, 1933), Chap. XII.

9. *The Protestant Era,* trans. James Luther Adams (Chicago: University of Chicago Press, 1948), p. 299.

10. Genesis 1:28. See also Brunner, *The Divine Imperative,* p. 195.

## Chapter Two

1. I Corinthians 2:14 (Authorized Version).

2. Psalm 36:9.

3. See Nicolas Berdyaev, *Truth and Revelation,* trans. R. M. French (New York: Harper, 1953).

4. Matthew 5:48.

5. Cited in Matthew Spinka, *Nicolas Berdyaev: Captive of Freedom* (Philadelphia: Westminster Press, 1950), p. 143.

6. Nicolas Berdyaev, *The Destiny of Man,* trans. Natalie Duddington (New York: Scribners, 1937), p. 377.

7. John 15:4–11. See also Colossians 1:27: "Christ in you, the hope of glory." It seems plausible to suppose that "glory" in this context connotes, not merely the eternal blessedness of the individual believer, but also, through it, the realization of the divine will for him, and thus the glorification of God.

8. John 17:3.

9. Romans 8:38–39.

10. II Corinthians 4:16–18.

11. *The Reawakening of Christian Faith* (New York: Macmillan, 1949), p. 124.

12. *Duino Elegies,* trans. J. B. Leishman and Stephen Spender (New York: W. W. Norton, 1939), Appendix IV, p. 28.

13. See Nicolas Berdyaev, *Solitude and Society,* trans. George Reavey (London: Goeffry Bles: Centenary Press, 1938).

*14. Dream and Reality,* trans. Katherine Lampert (New York: Macmillan, 1951), p. 181. See also *The Realm of Spirit and the Realm of Caesar,* trans. Donald A. Lowrie (New York: Harper, 1952), p. 37, and *The Destiny of Man,* p. 377.

*15. A Preface to Morals* (New York: Macmillan, 1929), pp. 181–183.

*16. Living Time and the Integration of the Life* (New York: Hermitage House, 1953), p. 120.

*17.* Ibid., p. 53.

*18.* Quoted by Rollo May, *Man's Search for Himself* (New York: Norton, 1935), p. 241.

*19.* See Gordon W. Allport, *Personality: A Psychological Interpretation* (New York: Holt, 1937), pp. 350–351.

*20.* See Berdyaev, *Solitude and Society,* p. 61.

*21.* See Reinhold Niebuhr, *An Interpretation of Christian Ethics,* p. 8 ff. and Chap. IV.

*22.* Matthew 18:20: "Where two or three are gathered together in my name, there am I in the midst of them."

*23.* Berdyaev, *Solitude and Society,* p. 166.

*24. Man's Search for Himself,* p. 246.

*25.* Reinhold Niebuhr, *The Nature and Destiny of Man* (New York: Scribners, 1949), I, 146–147.

## Chapter Three

*1. Human Destiny* (New York: New American Library, 1947), pp. 86–88.

*2. The Nature and Destiny of Man,* I, 181.

*3.* Ibid., pp. 182, 185.

*4.* Ibid., p. 242.

*5.* Brunner, *Man in Revolt,* p. 132 ff.

*6.* Brunner, *The Scandal of Christianity* (Philadelphia: Westminster, 1951), p. 64.

*7.* W. H. Auden, *The Age of Anxiety* (New York: Random House, 1947), pp. 29–30.

*8.* William Temple, *Christianity and Social Order* (Harmondsworth: Penguin Books, 1942), p. 38.

*9. Basic Writings of St. Augustine,* ed. Whitney J. Oates (New York: Random House, 1948), II, 818.

*10.* Brunner, *Man in Revolt,* p. 270.

*11.* Niebuhr, *An Interpretation of Christian Ethics,* p. 85.

*12.* Brunner, *Man in Revolt,* pp. 270–271.

*13.* See ibid., pp. 248 ff., and p. 250.

*14.* See ibid., Chap. ix, "The Unity of Personality and Its Decay."

*15.* For corroboration of the thesis that compulsive sexuality is frequently the symptom of some more profound psychic malorientation, see Otto Fenichel, *The Psychoanalytic Theory of Neurosis* (New York: Norton, 1945), pp. 515–523.

*16.* *The Nature and Destiny of Man,* i, 179.

*17.* Josiah Royce, *The Problem of Christianity* (Chicago: University of Chicago Press, 1968), p. 127.

*18.* See Joseph Fletcher, *Situation Ethics* (Philadelphia: Westminster Press, 1966), p. 65 ff.

*19.* *An Interpretation of Christian Ethics,* p. 77 ff.

*20.* See Calvin's *Commentary on Romans,* 2:14.

## Chapter Four

*1.* Isaiah 55:8–9.

*2.* Hosea 11:9.

*3.* Emil Brunner, *The Mediator,* trans. Olive Wyon (Philadelphia: Westminster Press, 1947), pp. 448, 447.

*4.* Romans 6:23.

*5.* *The Incarnation of the Word of God* (New York: Macmillan, 1951), p. 32.

*6.* *The Scandal of Christianity,* p. 79.

*7.* *Basic Christian Ethics* (New York: Scribners, 1954), p. 254.

*8.* *Christian Personal Ethics,* p. 228.

*9.* *The Principles of Christian Ethics* (New York: Abingdon-Cokesbury, 1943), pp. 130–131.

*10.* *Social Salvation* (New York: Scribners, 1935), pp. 94–95.

*11.* Ibid., p. 70.

*12.* Matthew 19:17, Mark 10:18, Luke 18:19.

*13.* *Christian Ethics and Moral Philosophy* (New York: Scribners, 1955), p. 52.

*14.* Ibid.

*15.* *Basic Christian Ethics,* pp. 249–264.

*16.* Søren Kierkegaard, *The Gospel of Suffering and the Lilies of the Field* (Minneapolis: Augsburg, 1948), pp. 211–212.

*17.* See Genesis 2, 3; Romans 7:18–19.

*18.* See Berdyaev, *Truth and Revelation,* Chap. III.

*19.* *A Theology for the Social Gospel* (New York: Abingdon, 1945), p. 177, pp. 242–273; "Ethical *Versus* Forensic Conceptions of Salvation," in *A Rauschenbusch Reader,* ed. Benson Y. Landis (New York: Harper, 1957), p. 135.

*20.* *Adversus haereses,* v. pref.

*21.* For a meaningful discussion of "covering" and "expiation," see Brunner, *The Mediator,* pp. 520–522.

*22.* *Situation Ethics,* p. 103.

*23.* *A Treatise on Christian Liberty* (Philadelphia: Muhlenberg Press, 1947), pp. 29–30.

*24.* Ramsey, *Basic Christian Ethics,* p. 355.

*25.* *Situation Ethics,* p. 105.

*26.* *An Interpretation of Christian Ethics,* p. 111.

*27.* *Types of Ethical Theory,* 2nd ed. (Oxford: Clarendon, 1886), II, 122–125.

*28.* Luke 2:49 (Authorized Version).

## Chapter Five

*1.* *Situation Ethics,* p. 44.

*2.* Ibid., p. 99.

*3.* *Basic Christian Ethics,* pp. 2–10.

*4.* See Isabel Patterson, *The God of the Machine* (New York: Putnams, 1943), pp. 90–91.

*5.* These passages are paraphrased in Henry Hazlitt, *The Foundations of Morality* (Princeton: Van Nostrand, 1964), pp. 19–20. The *Deontology* has been out of print since its original edition.

*6.* *A Treatise of Human Nature,* Bk. III, Pt. II, Sec. 2.

*7.* *Situation Ethics,* pp. 55, 134, 31.

*8.* *The Masks of Society* (New York: Appleton-Century-Crofts, 1966), p. 40.

*9.* *The Constitution of Liberty* (Chicago: University of Chicago Press, 1960), p. 77.

*10.* *On Liberty* (Chicago: Gateway Editions, n.d.), pp. 11–12.

*11.* William Ernest Hocking, *The Present Status of the Philosophy of Law and of Rights* (New Haven: Yale University Press, 1926), pp. 70–75 passim.

*12.* Ibid., p. 74.

*13. American Democracy and Natural Law,* p. 91.

*14. The Conservative Mind* (Chicago: Regnery, 1953), p. 42. See also William Graham Sumner, *What Social Classes Owe to Each Other* (Caldwell, Idaho: Caxton Printers, 1952), pp. 14–15.

*15.* See Charles W. Kegley and Robert W. Bretall, eds., *Reinhold Niebuhr: His Religious, Social, and Political Thought* (New York: Macmillan, 1956), pp. 434–436.

*16.* See the study produced by the Federal Council of Churches, *Christian Values and Economic Life* (New York: Harper, 1954), esp. pp. 212–217.

*17.* See John Ladd's introduction to Kant's *Metaphysical Elements of Justice,* trans. John Ladd (New York: Bobbs-Merrill, 1965), p. xi.

*18.* Isaiah Berlin, *Two Concepts of Liberty* (London: Oxford, 1958); J. L. Talmon, *The Origins of Totalitarian Democracy* and *Political Messianism* (New York: Praeger, 1960).

*19.* For a penetrating discussion of the distinction between freedom and the ends which freedom ought to serve, see Frank S. Meyer's *In Defense of Freedom* (Chicago: Regnery, 1962), esp. pp. 53–58 and 67–70.

*20.* R. H. Tawney, *The Acquisitive Society* (New York: Harcourt, Brace, 1920), Chap. ii.

*21.* Harold J. Laski, *A Grammar of Politics* (London: George Allen and Unwin, 1925), p. 91.

*22.* Ludwig von Mises, *Human Action* (New Haven: Yale University Press, 1949), Chap. xxvi.

*23. The Metaphysical Theory of the State* (London: George Allen and Unwin, 1918), pp. 35–36.

*24.* Herbert Spencer, *Principles of Ethics* (New York: Appleton, 1893), ii, 222.

*25.* Nicolas Berdyaev, *The Realm of Spirit and the Realm of Caesar,* trans. Donald A. Lowrie (New York: Harper, 1952), p. 99.

## Chapter Six

*1.* John Kenneth Galbraith, *The Affluent Society* (Boston: Houghton Mifflin, 1958).

*2. Reclaiming the American Dream* (New York: Random House, 1966), Chap. vi and passim.

*3. Democracy in America,* Pt. ii, Bk. 2, Sec. 3.

*4. The Good Society* (Boston: Little, Brown, 1937), p. 35.

*5.* See also Yale Brozen, "Is Government the Source of Monopoly?," *The Intercollegiate Review*, v (Winter 1968–69), 67–78.

*6.* See S. I. Benn and R. S. Peters, *The Principles of Political Thought* (New York: Free Press, 1965), pp. 264–265.

*7.* For a keen but inconclusive discussion of this issue, see J. Edward Bond, "Whose Rights?," *Modern Age,* xi (Summer 1967), 283–293.

*8. The Masks of Society,* p. 215.

*9. The Good Society,* pp. 308–309.

*10.* Cited ibid., p. 309.

*11.* For a critical analysis of the policy of occupational licensure, see Milton Friedman, *Capitalism and Freedom* (Chicago: University of Chicago Press, 1962), Chap. ix.

*12.* See von Mises, *Human Action,* p. 629.

*13. The Good Society,* p. 223.

*14.* Quoted in Irving Dilliard, ed., *One Man's Stand for Freedom: Mr. Justice Black and the Bill of Rights* (New York: Knopf, 1963), p. 477.

*15.* René de Visme Williamson, *Independence and Involvement: A Christian Reorientation in Political Science* (Baton Rouge: Louisiana State University Press, 1964), pp. 167–168.

*16.* "The Open Society and Its Fallacies," in Peter Radcliff, ed., *Limits of Liberty: Studies of Mill's "On Liberty"* (Belmont, Calif.: Wadsworth, 1966), p. 34.

*17.* Ibid.

*18. The Present Status of the Philosophy of Law and of Rights,* p. 90.

*19.* Steven B. Cord, *Henry George: Dreamer or Realist?* (Philadelphia: University of Pennsylvania Press, 1965), p. 231.

*20.* E. R. A. Seligman, *Essays in Taxation,* 9th ed. (New York: Macmillan, 1923), p. 71.

*21.* Cord, *Henry George: Dreamer or Realist?,* p. 83.

*22.* Spencer, *Principles of Ethics,* ii, 113.

*23. The Present Status of the Philosophy of Law and of Rights,* p. 88 ff.

*24. Social Statics* (New York: Appleton and Company, 1850), Chap. ix, Sec. 1.

*25.* Henry George, *A Perplexed Philosopher* (1892).

*26. Second Treatise of Government,* Chap. v, par. 27.

27. Henry George, *Progress and Poverty* (New York: Robert Schalkenbach Foundation, 1962), p. 334.

28. W. E. H. Lecky, *Democracy and Liberty* (London: Longmans, Green, 1896), II, 293–294.

29. *Poverty and the State* (London: Constable, 1930), p. 320.

30. *On Liberty,* p. 138 ff.

31. Syndicated column by Dr. Walter C. Alvarez, *Birmingham News,* December 3, 1966.

32. John Milton, "The Readie and Easie Way to Establish a Free Commonwealth," *Works* (New York: Columbia University Press, 1932), VI, 140.

33. *The Realm of Spirit and the Realm of Caesar,* pp. 112–113.

34. *The Fate of Man in the Modern World,* trans. Donald Lowrie (Milwaukee: Morehouse Publishing Company, 1933), p. 53.

35. *Christ and Culture* (New York: Harper, 1951), p. 197. The interior quotation is from Sir Edwyn Clement Hoskyns, *The Fourth Gospel.*

36. *The Social Crisis of Our Time* (Chicago: University of Chicago Press, 1950), p. 102.

37. *Essays on Freedom and Power,* p. 79.


## Chapter Seven

1. See Isaiah Berlin, *Two Concepts of Liberty,* pp. 41–47.

2. See John Plamenatz, *On Alien Rule and Self-Government* (London: Longmans, 1960), p. 133.

3. Brunner, *The Divine Imperative,* p. 246.

4. See Gregory Vlastos, "Justice and Equality," in Brandt, ed., *Social Justice,* p. 60.

5. *On Liberty,* pp. 135–136.

6. See his letter dated February 3, 1825, *The Writings of Thomas Jefferson,* ed. H. A. Washington (Washington: Taylor and Maury, 1834), VII, 397. The address of the letter is missing, but internal evidence suggests that it was written to Joseph C. Cabell.

7. Hayek, *The Constitution of Liberty,* p. 380.

8. *Capitalism and Freedom,* p. 93 ff.

9. *The Constitution of Liberty,* p. 381.

10. See William Graham Sumner, *What Social Classes Owe To Each Other* (Caldwell, Idaho: Caxton Printers, 1952), p. 141.

*11.* Henry Sidgwick, *The Principles of Political Economy,* 2nd ed. (London: Macmillan, 1887), p. 563.

*12.* See Walter J. Blum and Harry Kalven, Jr., *The Uneasy Case for Progressive Taxation* (Chicago: University of Chicago Press, 1953).

*13.* Cord, *Henry George: Dreamer or Realist?,* pp. 191–193.

*14. The American Commonwealth,* 2nd ed. (London: Macmillan, 1891), II, 452–453.

*15.* See Article 24 of the Universal Declaration.

# Index

An asterisk after a page number indicates that the subject is quoted on the page but not identified there other than by a numeral referring to the notes at the back of the book.